James B. Atkinson

Chow Chows

Everything About Purchase, Care,
Nutrition, Diseases, and Training

With Color Photographs by Outstanding Animal
Photographers, and Drawings by Michele Earle-Bridges

Consulting Editor: Matthew M. Vriends, PhD

BARRON'S

Photo Credits
Michele-Earle Bridges: page 10 bottom
D. J. Hammer: pages 10 top, 19, 20 top, 37, 55 bottom, back cover top left and bottom right.
M. Ridder: inside back cover
Wim van Vught: front cover, inside front cover, pages 9, 20 bottom, 38, 55 top, 56, back cover top right and bottom left.

About the Author

James B. Atkinson, PhD, was born in Hawaii in 1934 and began his career as a professor of English and comparative literature. Throughout his life his interest in dogs has been constant. His specific interest in and familiarity with chow chows began as a boy. Because of his instinct for dogs, his neighbors encouraged him to help them raise their chow puppy. Later, he learned how to groom and train chows for entry into AKC-sponsored dog shows. He brings this knowledge and experience to helping you raise your chow.

All inquiries should be addressed to:
Barron's Educational Series, Inc.
250 Wireless Boulevard
Hauppauge, NY 11788

International Standard Book No. 0-8120-3952-1

Library of Congress Catalog No. 88-22273

Library of Congress Cataloging-in-Publication Data

Atkinson, James B.
Chow chows.

    Bibliography
    Includes index.
    1. Chow chows (Dogs)   I. Title.
SF429.C5A96   1988   636.7'2
ISBN 0-8120-3952-1   88-22273

PRINTED IN HONG KONG

19 18

Advice and Warning

This book is concerned with buying, keeping, and raising chow chows. The publisher and the author think it is important to point out that the advice and information for chow chow maintenance applies to healthy, normally developed animals. Anyone who buys an adult chow chow or one from an animal shelter must consider that the animal may have behavioral problems and may, for example, bite without any provocation. Such anxiety-biters are dangerous for the owner as well as for the general public.

Caution is further advised in the association of children with a chow chow, in meetings with other dogs, and in exercising the dog without a leash.

Contents

Foreword

When you think about life with a dog, do you ever consider owning "a giant orange chrysanthemum" or "a magnificent scarlet pin cushion"? Probably not. Perhaps only an artist like Georgia O'Keefe could visualize a chow chow's head in these terms. But even if you have not envisioned a chow in this way, her description certainly captures the regal, exotic, and original beauty of the breed.

An attraction to beauty has always been part of the lure of the chow chow. The wave of fascination with "Chinoiserie" that swept late 18th- and early 19th-century France and England — from Chinese painting, to rugs, porcelain, and jewelry — also included the chow chow. In fact, the earliest reference to chows in English comes from the Reverend Gilbert White, rector of Selborne, a naturalist, and a writer. His *The Natural History and Antiquities of Selbourne in the County of Southhampton* published in 1789, includes the following description:

"My near neighbor, a young gentleman in the service of the *East-India* Company, has brought home a dog and a bitch of the *Chinese* breed from *Canton*; such as are fattened in that country for the purpose of being eaten; they are about the size of a moderate spaniel; of a pale yellow colour, with coarse bristling hairs on their backs; sharp upright ears, and peaked heads, which give them a very fox-like appearance. Their hind legs are unusually straight, without any bend at the hock or ham, to such a degree as to give them an awkward gait when they trot. When they are in motion, their tails are curved high over their backs like those of some hounds, and have a bare place each on the outside from the tip midway, that does not seem to be matter of accident, but somewhat singular. Their eyes are jet-black, small and piercing; the inside of their lips and mouths of the same colour, and their tongues blue. When taken out into a field, the bitch showed some disposition for hunting, and dwelt on the scent of a covey of partridges till she sprung them, giving her tongue all the time... [they] bark much in a short thick manner, like foxes; and have a surly, savage demeanour like their ancestors, which are not domesticated."

Throughout history, fanciers of the chow have admired as well as warily respected this breed. The chow's large head, leonine ruff, distinctive muzzle, and handsome coat make it truly special.

This manual will provide you with all the information you will need to give your chow proper care and attention. The first chapter discusses the preliminary items to consider before bringing your dog home — whether it be a puppy or a grown animal. The second chapter focuses on the supplies necessary for housing and caring for your chow. The third chapter discusses diet and general feeding tips, while the fourth chapter concentrates on understanding your dog in the context of the breed's history and growth patterns.

The next three chapters concern specific care issues: how to deal with the early weeks of your newly formed association; tips on grooming, traveling, breeding and birthing — if you decide to breed your bitch; care of a sick dog, including useful home health care techniques; preventive medicine; and timely advice for specific disorders. The final detailed chapter, on training your chow chow, is vitally important to both inexperienced and veteran owners. This chapter explains a program of socialization that will introduce your puppy or young dog to proper and rigorous practice sessions. The socialization of the chow is of particular concern because of the breed's unfortunate reputation among many people. Both the novice and the experienced chow owner will find new and pertinent ideas in this chapter.

The drawings by Michele–Earle Bridges will help you visualize aspects of daily care and training. The color photographs illustrate various aspects of the routines of chows.

It is fairly easy to purchase a chow and bring it home. Becoming an alert, responsible owner, however, will require some care and attention. This book will guide you every step of the way.

James B. Atkinson

Considerations Before You Buy

Is a Chow Chow the Right Dog for You?

The fact that you are reading this book implies that you are seriously considering purchasing a dog, and specifically a chow chow. Assuming this is the case, remember that you are about to commit yourself to a serious responsibility. The questions and issues raised in this chapter, therefore, deserve your attention.

Although chows are more popular now than they were ten years ago, you probably still cannot ask a neighbor or a relative the specific questions that may occur to you about the care and feeding of a chow. During the heyday of the chow's popularity in the Roaring Twenties, however, newspapers and illustrated magazines often contained pictures of chows accompanying the rich and famous—whether on Sunset Boulevard, Park Avenue, or the promenade in Newport. There was even a chow on Pennsylvania Avenue—President and Mrs. Calvin Coolidge were very attached to their black chow, Timmy. In those days, you probably could easily have found someone to answer your questions about chows.

Whether or not the chow chow is a popular, or even a chic, breed is certainly not necessarily the first question you should ask. However, you should find out if there is a nearby chapter of the Chow Chow Club of America so that you can get informed answers to your specific questions. The American Kennel Club (AKC), 51 Madison Avenue, New York, New York 10010 can send you the addresses of these chapters.

To familiarize yourself with the breed, especially if you do not know someone who owns a chow, you should attend a couple of dog shows. By paying careful attention to dogs in the show ring, you will observe really good chows. Thus, when you do select a dog, you will be able to make a more intelligent choice. You will also have first-hand knowledge of the breed's personality traits-especially those that surface when the dog is under pressure. Finally, who can better tell you what a chow is really like than someone who has lived with one?

There are, however, specific characteristics of chow chows that might help you decide if this is the breed for you. Chows are generally considered prompt, docile, and obedient. Their appearance will remind you of an imposing, majestic aristocrat. Their loyalty is unswerving and their commitment to safeguarding their owners and their families is unstinting. They are meticulously clean dogs who enjoy playing with adults and children, but who also can at times keep their own counsel. This sense of independence sometimes makes them indifferent to strangers. Their sense of loyalty includes other dogs they like and creates a pleasant gregariousness. By the same token, they can become unremittingly irascible with dogs they dislike.

If you do choose a chow chow, it will probably be because you admire its exceptional beauty, respect its alert intelligence, and welcome its special personality into your home. No doubt you will have been captivated by the dog's expression, which the official AKC standard describes as being "essentially dignified, lordly, scowling, discerning, sober, and snobbish — one of independence." Or you may be fascinated by the feature that distinguishes chows from all other purebred dogs — their blue-black tongues.

Before you decide to look for *your* chow, run through the following checklist. It concerns items that you need to consider about yourself before you begin your search: your personality, family situation, provisions for caring for the dog, ability to afford its care, and willingness to make a long-term commitment. Remember, chows are likely to live ten or more years.

You need both time and patience to devote to your dog. Exercise is important — not merely a run in the backyard, but an open field where your dog can run freely. Training is important so that your dog will heed your commands, and proper training requires a great deal of time and patience.

You and your family must determine whether

you can readily give the dog proper care. You need enough room inside and outside the house; the dog needs a place it can call its own with a bed and enough peace to rest easily. You should also have a definite outdoor area that the dog can get used to. If you rent, you need to know whether or not your lease permits large pets, and if not, whether or not the landlord will negotiate this issue.

You and your family also need to decide in advance who will have primary responsibility for the dog and who will be second in command. Because chows focus their attention mainly on one person, this issue must be decided early.

Finally, you and your family must agree on the extent to which you are willing to sacrifice for your dog. Remember, veterinary expenses and food bills add up — the latter could reach $50 a month. Vacations will require extra planning and often some compromises. Long vacations may become a memory; at the very least, you will have to budget the expense of kenneling the dog while you are away.

Although these points may seem self-evident, many people overlook them. Give them careful and honest thought before you begin the quest for your chow, and the chances are the two of you will live long and happy lives together.

A Puppy or an Older Dog?

Opinion is evenly divided on this question. People looking for a pet that will adapt itself to the household usually vote for the puppy, but many professionals emphatically favor the grown dog. Sound arguments can be offered for each of these positions.

The most obvious reason for choosing a puppy is to enjoy its growth and development from a clambering, playful puppy to a stately adult. Dogs, too, have their "magic years." Also, by choosing a puppy, you set the tone for training; you teach the dog to adjust to your household. Moreover, you can more readily assure that the dog receives proper medical attention, early shots and boosters, and a nutritious diet. This process brings a great deal of pleasure and gratification, but it also requires a lot of patience and perseverance.

Some professionals counter these arguments by pointing out several advantages of acquiring a grown dog. They particularly urge the first-time dog owner to select a dog that has had a good start in life. Thus, the owner avoids the inconvenience of the early, and often messy, stages of puppyhood. The owner also is assured that the dog has been trained adequately for obedience and behavior. Of course, this presupposes that the time spent under someone else's care was really time well spent; there are obvious risks in not knowing exactly what kind of training occurred and in what spirit it was given.

Generally speaking, dogs are anxious to please, so they will seek to adjust to a new family. Chow chows, however, experience the imprinting phase early in their lives; you will need judgment and love to help one find its place in your family hierarchy. For those crucial months, your household replaces the puppy's littermates, and making one's way in this new "pack" is difficult. If you should discover that your older chow has not been trained carefully, it will probably be harder to rectify bad habits, particularly those of a behavioral nature. If dangerous behavioral aberrations persist, the unfortunate but necessary step is to have a veterinarian put the dog down.

How to Choose a Puppy

Although some of the suggestions made here are useful to someone who purchases an older dog, let's assume that you have decided to start from the beginning — or as close to it as you can. You need to consider the age of the puppy, where to obtain it, the sex you prefer, and what to look for. These steps will help you succeed in the selection process.

Considerations Before You Buy

The Puppy's Age

Be wary if the seller is willing to let you have your chow before it is eight weeks old. The puppy needs this much time for weaning and for an introduction to solid food. If the puppy is ready for its new diet, your job will be easier because there is little likelihood that digestive problems will occur, even given the change of scene. On the other hand, you should not wait much longer than ten weeks to select your puppy, because that is the ideal time to begin training. Since you've decided to opt for puppyhood, it's better to start when the puppy is ready.

Children and adults need to learn how to hold a puppy: place one hand around the rib cage and support the rear end and rear paws with the other.

The Puppy's Sex

This is another issue that divides dog lovers into two camps. You will find staunch partisans for one sex or the other in terms of affection, fidelity, and intelligence. The fact is, however, that the dog's sex is not relevant to any of these issues. Your chow's affection for and fidelity to you is in no way related to its sex; you will find that chows demonstrate these emotions even for unkind owners. Generally speaking, chows are intelligent, so the important point to consider is the dog's genes, not its sex.

Nevertheless, there are two areas in which sex does make a real difference. Once you've decided about them, you can make your choice. There is a qualitative difference concerning the protective aggression characteristic of each sex: the male's sense of territorial imperative is high; your turf is his turf. On the other hand, the female's need to protect is directed more toward other people and animals, because she believes that they represent a threat to you. A related point is that you will need to be more tolerant when walking a male chow. He will want to sniff at many more locations in order to mark his territory.

A second area in which consideration of sex differences is important is the female's heat. Your chow's first season can occur at any point from her seventh to eighteenth month. It lasts for about three weeks, and the cycle repeats itself at about six-month intervals. This topic will be discussed in more detail in Chapter 5. At this point you need to consider the extent of your patience in terms of two inevitable factors. First, there will be a discharge that may continue for several days and might stain your rugs; second, a clamorous press of males will camp for several days in your yard or hover around your doors.

Where to Buy

Here is a rule to follow: spend more time looking for your chow rather than more money buying it. Newspaper advertisements can get you on your way, but be sure to avoid puppy farms or large kennels that offer many different breeds. There you will usually find people more interested in profits than in dogs. In addition, you are more likely to find puppies without much human contact. The result can be a chow that will be shy or have another behavior problem. Ask the Chow Club of America or the American Kennel Club of America for a list of registered breeders in your area. A reputable dealer can also be a good source.

The more breeders you visit to observe dogs and kennel conditions, the more knowledgeable your final selection will be. This advice may be irritating, especially to your children, who will probably want to purchase a puppy at the first litter you visit. Nevertheless, it is worth heeding. If you are more comfortable with a pet store, make sure it is clean and ethically run. Also, find out as much information as you can about the actual breeding of the litter you are considering.

Breeding dogs is a complicated procedure, but you need to know something about how it is done so that you can intelligently choose a chow puppy. Breeders refer to dogs as being outbred, inbred, or linebred. Outbreeding means that the dogs are of the same breed, but are in no way related to one another. It insures that dogs are purebred chows, but it leaves the question of dominant and recessive genes to chance. Inbred dogs are those bred from within the same immediate family, so that a male could be bred with its daughter, sister, or mother and a bitch could be bred with her son, brother, or father. Although this method insures breed conformation and seeks to transmit the best genes, it cannot promise the latter. A linebred chow is one whose dam (mother) and sire (father) were of the same blood line but never from the same litter or even the previous generation. This is the ideal bloodline for your chow puppy. In order to determine what breeding procedures have been followed, you need to see the puppy's AKC pedigree. In most cases, this will not be prepared by the time a puppy is eight weeks old, but you can determine the lines by first comparing the AKC litter registration with the pedigrees of the puppy's dam and sire. A competent breeder will have this information readily available for you and will be glad to explain it to you.

What to Look For

When you first encounter a moving, yelping mass of energetic puppies, it's hard not to find each one alert, active, and adorable. Look more closely, however. Once you find a puppy that seems delighted by your voice or other attention-getting device, look carefully at its coat, and then examine its eyes, ears, nose, and throat. Also make sure that there are no unusual sniffles, wheezes, or coughs. The coat should be shiny, not scaly or patchy. These conditions might signal a skin disease. A sure sign that the breeder is not careful is a dirty or smelly coat. There should be no runny, mucous fluid in its eyes or dripping from its nose. The inside of the ears should be clean, smooth, and pink. The gums, too, should be pink and firm, supporting bright white teeth, not yellowish or discolored ones.

Be wary, too, if the breeder is willing to sell you the puppy before it is eight weeks old or unwilling to give you two very important documents. Eight weeks is the standard time frame to allow for proper growth, and it also allows time for completion of the paper work. The documents include dated proof that the puppy has been wormed. This is usually done once a litter is weaned, during the puppy's fifth or sixth week. You should also receive dated proof that the puppy has been inoculated against distemper, hepatitis, and leptospirosis. These are lethal diseases to puppies, but they inherit immunity from their mother for about six weeks. By the way, the first permanent shot against these fatal diseases will be your responsibility. Check with your veterinarian for the appropriate time — usually between ten and twelve weeks.

Finally, you should observe the interaction of the puppies in order to judge their temperaments. It is important to note not only how they get along

Motherhood is a time of pride (above) as well as vigilance (below).

with their littermates, but also how they interact with their dam, their breeder, and, of course, you and your family members. Try to strike a balance between the liveliest and the most docile puppy in the litter. Some puppies are wary of strangers, although that may often mean they are merely prudent rather than basically shy. Play with the puppies and, by rousing their curiosity, find out who leads the pack and who hangs behind. The former will probably be a rewarding handful of a chow, whereas the latter may be timid or shy. These are not desirable traits in a puppy, despite what your children may think or what your heart may tell you. Puppies that are instinctively shy have difficulty developing more outgoing personalities. They may grow up to be yapping, nipping piddlers—or worse, recalcitrant dogs or those that bite out of fear.

In the final analysis, you will probably find that the puppy chooses you. At least, you ought not to force yourself on it. And, in terms of what to look for, that may be the most important criterion of all.

Initial and Maintenance Costs

It is difficult to be very precise about costs. However, you should divide your expenses into these areas: purchase, licenses, insurance, food, veterinary care, and dog club membership fees.

You can pay as little as $200 for a chow, but one from good bloodlines can cost $600 or more. This is a significant investment; therefore, if a good pedigree is important to you because you plan to show and/or breed your chow, you must be prepared to spend this amount.

Above: Even while puppies prepare to set out for the world, they also need their mother's nurture. These puppies are not indifferent to being photographed, it's merely that their eyes haven't opened yet.
Below: Training is a constant responsibility, regardless of age.

Once you get the dog home, you will have several financial responsibilities. You must license the dog with your local municipality. Often, urban and suburban communities charge more than rural ones, and female dogs are usually more expensive to register. The reason is simple: the potential profit from a bitch is greater than that from a male. You pay for that possibility, whether or not you intend to breed your bitch. It follows, therefore, that a spayed bitch is less expensive to license. Also, you should consider the insurance liability dogs represent; they can be at fault for numerous reasons, from causing an accident, to biting an adult or child, to damaging property. Some dog owners even take out a health or life insurance policy — or both. A final responsiblity concerns licensing your chow. In addition to wearing the tag provided by your local agency, your dog should wear a veterinarian's tag, a tattoo, or some visible proof that it has been immunized for rabies, distemper, and leptospirosis.

By far the greatest costs are those for food and veterinary care. Depending upon the kind of food you buy, a chow's monthly food bill can be $50 or higher. Veterinary bills are equally hard to predict because they will vary according to the types of services required and whether or not your community is a rural one.

A Final Word

As you leave for home with your new friend, remember that its first few days with you will be its most difficult. Remember that your dog is leaving the security of its surroundings; a puppy is leaving the security of its mother and the camaraderie of its littermates. See if there is a toy or familiar object that you can take with you to ease the transition into your house. Should you meet your puppy at a very early age — before it is appropriate to take it home with you — there are two things you can do to facilitate the transition. You can leave the puppy a towel or a toy with your scent on it so that you can take it home along with the puppy. In addition, if you live close enough to the puppy to visit it, do so as frequently as possible. Cuddle it, handle it, pet it, and talk to it as often as you can. Both of these suggestions will pay off handsomely by creating a better bonding with your puppy.

Supplies and Housing

Whether it be a grown dog or a puppy, your chow will need some basic feeding and grooming equipment as well as clearly demarcated living areas. You should have some of these items on hand before the puppy's arrival, and you should think about its living, playing, and sleeping areas in advance. It's never too early to begin planning for that day.

Basic Equipment

Your chow's food dish should be large enough and heavy enough to last a long while. Food dishes come in a variety of materials — plastic, earthenware, and metal. Because your dog will ultimately weigh around 50 pounds (23 kg), you will need one heavy enough so that the dog cannot slide it all over the floor. Some dishes even come with a rubber ring on the bottom to retard movement. You could, of course, always add one of these later, after you begin to find your dog's dish nudged into hard-to-get-at areas underneath the kitchen table or counter.

During your dog's lifetime it will need several kinds of collars. A puppy needs an ordinary leather or nylon collar, but a grown chow needs something more substantial and of medium width. Leather is a good bet except that it tends to fall apart with exposure to the elements. Bear in mind that you do not want to irritate or harm your chow's leonine ruff. Consequently, many owners remove the collar when the dog is around the house so as not to damage the ruff.

You will also need a choke collar when you begin serious training. This is usually a steel chain, although some are of braided nylon or leather, materials that may do less harm to the ruff. This kind of collar will tighten around the dog's neck when you tug on the lead attached to it, thereby providing a clear signal — an incentive — to obey your command. Some people find a spurred or prong collar better for training. If you decide on this type of collar because your dog needs an added incentive, be sure to remove it immediately following the training session.

Choke collars (top) are ideal for training your chow chow. Leather collars (bottom left) and nylon collars (bottom right) are also serviceable for everyday use.

Food and water bowls. Choose bowls that are sturdy and heavy enough to remain stable while an eager chow chow is eating or drinking.

Once you have determined the area in which you are likely to walk your chow and how much freedom it should have during walks, you can decide on the length of your leash, or, more properly, lead. These, too, come in various materials.

Leashes with various types of fasteners: the safety catch (left), the spring clip (center), and the spring catch (right).

The retractable lead is convenient for giving your chow flexibility of movement.

Webbed canvas cloth is common, but length is the major concern. A short lead is useful for walking in areas where you want to keep your dog near you at all times. You may want to consider buying a long lead that has a reel built into it that expands and retracts as your dog moves about. You can control the distance with a button on the grip of the reel, thus achieving greater freedom of movement for yourself and your dog. These leads extend to about 30 feet (9 m) and are very handy. Because the strain on a lead occurs near the dog's end, some leads come with a chain about a foot long (30 cm) linking the clip to the lead itself. This is not a very useful device for young dogs because they are likely to chew on this readily accessible part and do permanent harm to their teeth. Finally, if your lead is not equipped with reflective tape, buy some and wrap it around your lead. This added safety feature will be valuable for night-time walks.

Some owners feel more comfortable if they have a muzzle — especially for use on long trips, in exploring territory that is new to the dog, or on trips to the veterinarian. Remember to purchase one that will adjust to your dog as it develops from a puppy into adulthood.

Good citizenship is enhanced by purchasing a pooper-scooper, either hinged or unhinged, and with a handle appropriate for your height. Most urban and suburban localities now require dog owners to clean up after their dogs. Even if your community has not yet passed such legislation, your neighbors will be very grateful to you for having been considerate enough of their property to buy and use one. You may also find it handy for cleaning up your own yard.

Be sure to attach an identification tag to your dog's collar, either a round one that can be affixed with an S-hook or a flat one that can be riveted onto the dog's collar. In addition to your name, address, and telephone number, be sure to include your area code in case you are separated from your dog at some distance from your home. There is some disagreement about the advisability of including the dog's name on the tag. Chances are, however, that your chow will not cuddle up to strangers. Therefore, if people can make your frightened,

Supplies and Housing

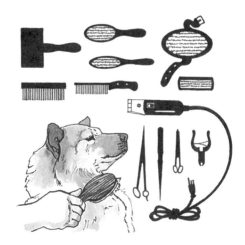

Some useful grooming equipment.

lonely dog more at ease by calling it by name, why not add it to the dog's tag?

In order to groom your chow properly, you will need a variety of implements. (For grooming techniques and procedures, see Chapter 5.) First, get a large wire slicker brush that has teeth slightly bent so that it can both clean the dog's coat and help remove scales. You will also need a long pin brush, made from either wire or rubber, with smooth, rounded pins. A dog rake is also a good idea, particularly if your chow runs through fields or if you are somewhat lax about your grooming schedule. This handy tool has two rows of teeth shaped in a "V" for combing through the dog's coat and picking apart matted snarls. If you learn to do it properly, you can trim your dog's nails once you have the proper clipper. If you are wary of this task, ask your veterinarian to do it. Finally, for fluffing out the ruff and coat, you will need a comb with fairly long teeth, 1.5 inches (4 cm), set at ¼-inch intervals (.6 cm).

One final concern for which you will need some equipment is the control and treatment of fleas, ticks, and parasites. A good pair of tweezers will help you pluck out ticks and other parasites. Fleas can become a major problem. Since an infestation of fleas wreaks havoc with a household, take precautionary measures early in the season. You can buy insecticidal sprays and a pyrethrin dip to help counteract fleas, ticks, lice, and ear mites once they begin to plague your dog—and you. There are flea combs, some of which dispense a chemical that will saturate the dog's coat and skin while you comb its coat. Your supermarket carries ordinary flea collars, though veterinarians often advise against them for reasons ranging from ineffectiveness to harm. An extremely effective ultrasonic collar equipped with a lithium battery is now available. These collars emit tiny blasts of ultrasound that maintain a protective zone around your dog. Although this invention may seem like something from science fiction, it does a good job of keeping fleas off your dog from the start. For further advice on dealing with fleas (see pages 54, 57).

Proper Toys

Playing with your dog or watching it play is one of the greatest pleasures of having a dog. It's a good idea to have a few toys ready for your new dog, but be sure to buy ones made of proper materials. Many toys also help the dog strengthen its teeth and jaw muscles. Making toys available allows the bored or lonely puppy — or dog — an opportunity to chew off its aggressions if you are not around to divert it.

Chow chow puppies do well with hard rubber balls, rings, bones, or pull toys. Rawhide bones are a good idea, too, because they help to keep tartar from forming on the dog's teeth. The only problem with rawhide is that your chow will soon chew it into small pieces. When the bone gets to that stage, throw away the small pieces so that your dog does not swallow them and choke. A good form of exercise for both you and your dog is provided by aerodynamically designed discs; you can throw them and teach your dog to catch and retrieve them.

Supplies and Housing

Regardless of the toy, bone, or disc you buy, it is crucial to consider the materials that constitute it. Most wooden toys splinter, and most chows can easily destroy plastic. A good pet supply store will carry a variety of toys made out of hard rubber or synthetic materials that will not disintegrate too rapidly and thus be safe for your pet.

There are two sides to the issue of whether or not to give your dog real bones. To be avoided at all costs are bones that can splinter and harm the mouth, throat, or entire digestive tract. For this reason, chicken and pork bones are notoriously bad. Many people favor strong marrow bones; however, too many bones, or bones supplied too often, tend to produce constipation. Moreover, not everyone agrees about whether or not to cook the bones before you offer them to your dog. If you decide on marrow bones, you could look for a pet supply store carrying natural, sterilized USDA-inspected bones.

Of course, sometimes a toy is not, in fact, a toy at all. This concern comes up mainly with puppies, but it can also be a problem with grown dogs. Old sneakers, shoes, slippers, socks, and sweaters, especially if they have your scent on them, are particularly delectable treats. Obviously, you should never give any of these discarded items to your dog to play with. It cannot distinguish a discarded item from a treasured one. And that can only mean trouble. If, for example, you give your chow an old slipper, you will probably be delighted by your pet's antics as it growls at and chews the unwanted item. Your feelings will change dramatically when you discover that your chow has also adopted your *new* slippers as a toy. A little forethought will help you avoid this situation.

You should also have treats readily available. They are a good way to reward your chow for learning something you have taught it or for tolerating the grooming process. Treats come in all sizes, shapes, and flavors; they offer another opportunity for keeping your dog's teeth clean. At the outset, only *one person* should hand them out—the family member who is primarily responsible for the pet.

Sleeping and Feeding Areas in the House

It is important to establish a regular routine for your puppy as soon as possible. Just as an orderly environment is best for a child, so is it for puppies and dogs. A regular routine helps them adapt better to the new conditions that you and your household represent. Establish a feeding schedule that fits easily into your routine. The puppy can then expectantly anticipate its food and be fulfilled without undue disruption of your life. Since it should always be fed in the same location, decide on a place that will allow easy cleanups. You will probably find that your puppy is none too meticulous about the floor surrounding its dish — either now or as it grows older. So a linoleum- or tile-covered area is best.

In setting up its sleeping arrangements, there are several considerations. First, especially while the puppy is still young, you need a place that is neither too hot nor too drafty. Second, choose a place that is not too close to the main traffic patterns in your house, but not so far removed that your puppy cannot keep abreast of the latest household developments. The best way for it to feel at home is to know who is where and what is going on. However, for it to be healthy and active, it needs to be able to get sufficient rest.

You can build the bed yourself or you can purchase it in a pet store. You can even go to an import store and find something in rattan that, although not originally intended to hold a chow chow, does the job adequately. Pads for the bed range from cedar-filled, to plush, to blankets and pillows. Cedar-filled pads or mattresses, in addition to having a pleasant, woodsy smell, also are a natural deterrent to external parasites. Blankets will do as well, but avoid plastic. If you decide to build a bed, select a wood that will not splinter and finish it off with a nontoxic stain; avoid varnish. You might consider these dimensions, remembering that you will need to make an insert for a board

Supplies and Housing

Sleeping box and baskets. Make certain you choose one that is large enough for a full-grown chow chow to lie down in comfortably.

regions. Although you may think that coat is too oppressive to endure, it serves as insulation for your dog. Thus, do not cut it off because you mistakenly believe that your chow would be cooler without it. As long as you provide adequate shade and cool drinking water nearby, your chow should adapt to any climate.

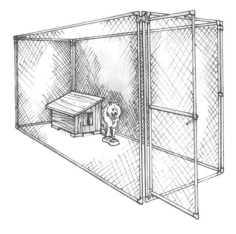

A dog run is a good place for your chow to get fresh air and exercise and to develop independence.

down the middle while your puppy grows into its bed: 36 × 24 × 8 inches (91 × 61 × 20 cm).

During the early stages of having a puppy around the house, many people find that hauling out a baby pen from the attic or using a safari cage helps give the puppy a sense of security as well as a protected place to view all the action. However, such a cage should not be used for very long periods of time. Puppies need to exercise freely and to be able to relieve themselves readily. A couple of hours at a time is not too long, and you will find cleaning up a playpen is easier than cleaning up a larger area.

An Outdoor Run

Chow chows are cold-weather dogs. They thrive on cold and snow, but they do not enjoy walking on dewy grass or wet sidewalks. In fact, most chows hate rain. As for warm climates, they certainly adapt to them well, too. You will probably find, however, that they shed their generally heavy coat in warmer

You can make your dog's life outside more comfortable in several ways. If you are handy with tools, build a fenced-in yard for your dog. Because setting the posts is a complicated procedure, you may want to enlist somebody to help — or even to do the entire job. This kind of pen provides a good place for your dog to move about rather freely — at least in terms of your need to supervise it. The dog gets fresh air and exercise, which fosters its sense of independence. Nevertheless, do not offend your chow's sense of dignity by keeping it penned up for a long time. A chow has a great need to feel it is a valued and treasured part of your household. Just as it needs exercise, it needs time with you and your family to assure it of its place in your "pack."

Supplies and Housing

Furthermore, be sure to introduce the idea of staying outside — for whatever length of time — gradually. You can show your chow that you consider its yard an adjunct of your house by occasionally feeding it there and also by playing with it there for a while. Once it has reconciled itself to remaining in the pen for an hour or two, your dog will grow accustomed to it and will delight in the smells that abound there. Then it will be ready to stay for longer stretches of time. Despite the chow's tolerance for cold, it is not advisable to leave a puppy or a new dog outside all night if it is very cold—or if there are any signs of sickness.

An appropriate dog house increases your chow's comfort outside. The hinged roof makes it easier for you to clean and air it.

You can also make your dog's stay outside more comfortable by constructing, or having constructed, a doghouse. Make sure you create a house in which your fully grown chow not only can stand up easily, but can also stretch out comfortably. However, don't make it so large that the dog's body heat cannot keep it cozy. Also give some consideration to the roof. On the one hand, it needs to be secure enough to protect your dog from rain and cold; on the other hand, a hinged roof will allow you to clean the house out easily with hot water and a disinfectant. Although you need a door and perhaps, in warmer regions, a window, climate conditions will dictate the construction of these openings. One of the greatest threats to your dog's well-being is the heartworm parasite, carried by certain mosquitoes. Therefore, it is important to screen these openings whenever practical. In colder regions, attach a blanket or piece of rug over the door. (For additional information about the dangerous parasite that causes this deadly disease, see the discussion on page 54.)

When selecting a permanent location for the house, avoid an area exposed fully to the sun or one that is constantly damp. Position the house so that it is protected from the prevailing winds. Finally, raise the house off the ground so that ground moisture will not seep in through the floor. Inserting straw, leaves, or garden mulch will provide additional insulation.

Now that you have provided your chow chow with basic equipment and living areas, you are ready to consider its nutritional needs.

The tradition and history of the breed enable the chow chow to be particularly in tune with nature. This chow chow, obviously vacationing with its master, seems to take both the vastness of a mountain meadow and the excitement of a rushing stream easily in stride.

The Proper Diet

It is a shocking truth that most dog owners' feeding habits do their pets more harm than good. At one extreme, there is the indulgent feeder of treats, desserts, or hors d'oeuvres. At the other extreme, there is the bargain-hunter who buys nothing but prepared food that is on sale at the local supermarket. Some owners proudly proclaim, "My dog eats exactly what I eat." Of course, some people find the subject of nutrition too dull to be of any interest.

You will probably be surprised by your chow's capacity for food. It is actually less than you might expect — less, even, than that of many smaller dogs. Since this is the case, you must make sure that what your chow eats is of good quality and sufficient for its nutritional needs. Failure to do so can result in severe health problems, ranging from serious loss or gain in weight, to inadequate bone growth and cartilage formation, to skin diseases, and to blood disorders.

Taking command of the dietary situation means insuring that what your chow eats will be metabolized into the proper amount of energy, measured in terms of calories. Calories release the energy into your dog's body so that it can perform all of its necessary life functions. You can accomplish this goal either by preparing your chow's food yourself or by being a careful purchaser of commercially prepared food. Whichever method you choose, you are seeking the proper balance of nutritional components so that your dog can realize its full physical potential, develop its capacity for intelligence, and be temperamentally stable.

Camaraderie is a hallmark of the breed — whether it exists between a boy and his new puppy (above) or a young woman and her full grown chow chow. (below).

Components of a Proper Diet

Protein is doubtless the most important component of your dog's diet. It forms the basis of all the body's tissues and helps repair them during an illness or after an accident. When combined with calcium, protein contributes to the growth of teeth, bones, muscles, and skin. Protein is also necessary to maintain the amino acid supply because dogs produce only 13 of the 23 necessary acids. At least 20 percent or more of a dog's ration should be protein; lean meat and egg whites are more complete protein sources than are soy, peas, or beans.

Protein is also found in beef. Whether it is cooked or not makes no nutritional difference, although cooking meat removes some of the vitamins. With all the bones removed, pork and fish are good sources for increasing your dog's protein intake. But because of their potential for causing virus infections and diseases in dogs, they must always be cooked before being offered as part of the diet. You can occasionally serve liver and kidney, but the heart, a good source of muscle protein, can be a more consistent part of the diet. It should be boiled and diced before serving. As for chicken, if all the bones are removed and it, too, is cooked, it provides an easily digestible, nourishing meal, especially for an ill or recuperating dog.

Recently, fats have drawn our attention as another necessary component of a dog's diet. In addition to providing energy, fats help dogs to grow, remain active, and receive proper insulation. Fatty acids also energize the metabolic process. If you want to enhance your chow's glossy coat, remember that fatty acids are necessary for developing both the cell structure and the good skin tissue that contribute to a healthy coat. Beef and lamb contain saturated fatty acids, so you will need to supplement them with soft and liquid fats found in lard, poultry fat, horsemeat, liver, fish, corn oil, and other vegetable oils. Your chow's need for fat will vary depending upon its activity level as well as its age and size, but a 10 to 15 percent level is good to maintain.

The Proper Diet

This diagram of your chow's internal organs shows you how your dog processes its food.

1. Esophagus
2. Lung
3. Liver
4. Stomach
5. Small intestine
6. Large intestine
7. Anus

The Proper Diet

A third important nutritional component for your chow is the variety of protein-extending carbohydrates found in sugars, starches, and cellulose. These are excellent, though short-term, energy sources. Your dog can get them in corn, cornmeal, rice, cereals, and beet pulp. Fiber is a complex carbohydrate that aids digestion and elimination. Try to keep the carbohydrate level of the diet low, 5 to 10 percent. Although some of the excess is stored in the liver and muscles, your dog will soon become chubby if its diet contains too many starchy foods. If carbohydrates are not processed correctly, they are virtually indigestible and can cause diarrhea.

A vitamin balance is another important component, but the emphasis is on *balance*; either a deficiency or an excess can be harmful. As in humans, vitamins help dogs resist disease, act as catalysts for enzyme functioning, and provide a regular metabolism. Some specific vitamins are important. Vitamin A helps skin and coat formation, prevents infections, and promotes bone growth. It is found in organ meats, such as liver, and in cheese. Vitamin E helps in reproduction and lactation, in calming excitable dogs, and in maintaining good muscle tone. Because balance is the watchword and because a healthful diet usually contains sufficient vitamins, consult your veterinarian before adding a vitamin supplement to your chow's diet.

We know of at least 20 minerals that act as important catalysts, promote the proper development of teeth, bones, and hair, and maintain proper body-fluid balance. For example, calcium and phosphorus, found in animal bones and gristle, are essential for teeth; copper and iron, for blood hemoglobin; and iodine, for growth. Again, however, balance is important; traces of these minerals plus manganese, cobalt, zinc, and boron exist in all foods. So, again, consult your veterinarian before deciding to add minerals to your dog's diet.

Finally, water is an absolutely vital dietary component. No dog can live without it because it carries nutrients throughout the body, helps digestion and food absorption, and flushes away waste materials. Although some commercially prepared food is high in water — almost 75 percent — soak the dry, kibble variety in water before serving it. Furthermore, a fresh supply of water at room temperature in a clean dish should be constantly and readily available to your dog.

Commercial vs. Household Foods

If, after reading the preceding section, you are still willing to devote the time necessary for preparing your chow's food, bear in mind that maintaining the proper interaction among all the nutritional components requires considerable attention. Should you decide to rely on commercially prepared food, however, you will discover numerous options. Well-established, nationally known firms generally maintain close quality control over their products. You can, therefore, rely on them, although you should check labels to verify the proportions of nutritional components included in various prepared foods. Also, remember that you can add vegetables, greens, and starches to the commercial foods in order to maintain the proper carbohydrate level.

One type of commercial food is *canned dog food*. The labels indicate the mixture of protein, fat, carbohydrates, vitamins, and minerals contained in each can. These products are designed as nutritionally complete dog food. You may be dismayed at the high percentage of water in these foods — often around 75 percent but many people like the idea of offering meat and meat by-products directly to their pets.

Another option is *semi-moist dog food*; it contains only about 25 percent moisture, and it, too, is a complete, nutritionally sound food. One advantage is that it provides more energy per unit weight than does canned food. Because it contains less water, you must make sure your dog's water dish is always full.

The third option is *dry dog foods*, which actually contain about 10 percent water. Thus, they offer even more energy per unit weight than do the other

The Proper Diet

two choices. Needless to say, you must keep your dog's water dish full if you select this option.

In order to help you better plan your chow chow's feeding schedule, you need some specific information about *kilocalories*. When we talk about energy per unit weight in discussing various commercially prepared foods, we are really talking about kilocalories. A kilocalorie (also called *large calorie* or, simply, *calorie*) is used by nutritionists to measure the energy-producing value of food oxydized by the body. Assuming the average chow chow weighs from 40 to 60 pounds (18 to 27 kg), then a 50-pound (23 kg) dog will need about 990 calories a day to maintain good health, and a seven- to ten-month-old puppy will need about 1980 kilocalories to encourage growth. The following examples will help you calculate a typical daily ration:

• A puppy from weaning to three months should be fed four times a day, assuming a weight of 6 to 12 pounds (3 to 5 kg), so that it consumes 600 to 900 calories a day. At each sitting this means 6 to 8 ounces (170 to 227 g) of dry food, 2 to 4 ounces (57 to 113 g) of semi-moist food, and from 8 to 10 ounces (227 to 283 g) of canned food.

• A puppy from three to five months should be fed three times a day, assuming a weight of 12 to 25 pounds (5 to 11 kg), so that it consumes 960 to 1650 calories a day. At each feeding this means 8 to 14 ounces (227 to 397 g) of dry food, 4 to 6 ounces (113 to 170 g) of semi-moist food, and 10 to 19 ounces (283 to 539 g) of canned food.

• A puppy from five to seven months should be fed twice a day, assuming a weight of 20 to 35 pounds (9 to 16 kg), so that it consumes 1400 to 2170 calories a day. At each feeding this means 18 to 28 ounces (510 to 794 g) of dry food, 8 to 14 ounces (227 to 397 g) of semi-moist food, and 22 to 35 ounces (624 to 992 g) of canned food.

• A puppy from seven to ten months should be fed twice a day, assuming a weight of 25 to 40 pounds (11 to 18 kg), so that it consumes 1650 to 2500 calories a day. At each feeding this means 26 to 32 ounces (737 to 907 g) of dry food, 10 to 15 ounces (283 to 425 g) of semi-moist food, or 26 to 40 ounces (737 to 1134 g) of canned food.

• A grown chow of 50 pounds (23 kg) should be fed once a day so that it consumes 1350 calories a day. This means 35 ounces (992 g) of dry food, 16 ounces (454 g) of semi-moist food, or 42 ounces (1191 g) of canned food.

Consequently, if you decide to depend mainly on commercially prepared food, a good compromise is to supplement the dry or semi-moist kind with a helping of the canned type—but don't forget the full water dish. Tap water is, after all, the least expensive nutrient.

Feeding a Puppy

As the preceding sections indicate, a puppy's nutritional needs are quite different from those of a grown dog. Before you leave the breeder or pet store with your puppy, ask for a feeding schedule and a chart of ideal weekly growth. Each breeder has a particular schedule that rarely resembles anyone else's. If the chart is designed for chows, however, you have a reasonably accurate figure to guide you. Furthermore, each puppy grows at its own rate. It will be impossible to figure out in advance what that rate will be; all you can rely on are various rules of thumb. At each stage, however, you need to monitor your puppy's growth. You also need to determine the quantity, frequency, and quality of the food.

To determine how much you should feed your puppy, weigh it each week and compare that weight with a breed chart. Or you can follow a rule many breeders use: increase the daily amount 5 to 10 percent weekly. Since you want a lean chow, rely on the old adage, "the eye of the owner feeds the dog." It is probably better to err on the side of less food rather than more. Because puppies delight so in their food, it is easier and more fun to overfeed one. But if you want to be a responsible owner, let common sense be your guide — with a little trial and error for good measure.

How often you feed the puppy depends on its age. The schedule provided in the preceding section gives some guidelines to follow until the tenth or twelfth month. A grown Chow may be fed once a day, if convenient, or you can continue to feed it twice daily — but serve smaller portions.

What you feed is a matter of personal choice— combined with a consultation with your veterinarian. The wide variety of nutritionally balanced, commercially prepared puppy chows, puppy meals, and puppy foods should satisfy even the most finicky owner and puppy. If you want to prepare your own food, make sure you provide plenty of meat (such as ground beef, diced chicken, or veal), eggs, milk, and cottage cheese. At least two-thirds of the puppy's diet should be these protein-rich foods. The other third can include cereal mush — not so thick that it sticks in your dog's throat — rice, cornmeal, or fresh, finely chopped vegetables such as spinach, celery, carrots, or tomatoes.

During this period of your puppy's life, diet is of paramount importance. You should maintain vigilant and responsible attention. If your chow skips an occasional meal or leaves food in the dish when it usually gobbles it down voraciously, do not panic. Often it is your dog's way of saying, "That's enough for today. My stomach is upset." On the other hand, one sure indication that something is amiss is an extended period of a dog's being off its feed. Then, be sure to check with your veterinarian.

Finally, one test for proper diet and general health is observation of a dog's stool. A loose, mushy stool or diarrhea often signals that the dog's food has gone through the intestinal tract unprocesssed (for example, the protein may be of a poor quality), whereas a large stool often means the diet contains too much fiber or other indigestible items.

Feeding a Mature Dog

As your chow grows older, you will find that less activity requires less food. Just at the point where you may be prepared to spoil your dog by overfeeding, you must be sure not to. In fact, you may even have to stimulate its activity in order to encourage proper metabolism of the food eaten. It is up to you to determine its ideal weight. Your experience will tell you what is too fat or too thin, what its activity level is, and what its temperament is — a high-strung dog consumes more calories than does a placid one.

Calories are only one factor to consider reducing. Since overweight creates an undue strain on the dog's internal systems, you may shorten the dog's lifespan by not cutting its calorie intake. Fats, too, need to be reduced because they are harder for the older dog to digest and are high in calories. Although protein is important for an older dog, don't overload the liver and kidneys by feeding the wrong kind of protein. Too much meat or poor-quality protein does just that, so think of adding milk, cottage cheese, boiled egg, or cooked ground meat to its diet. Nephritis is quite common among older dogs, so ask your veterinarian for specific advice about protein foods. Also ask for recommendations about vitamin and mineral supplements at this age. Older dogs need more of both but the proper balance is essential; for example, calcium and phosphorus in a 1.2 to 1 ratio are necessary for an older dog's bones. A consultation with your veterinarian, however, is your best bet.

General Feeding Tips

• Since your chow respects regularity, try to feed it in the same place at the same time every day. If you realize that a permanent change in feeding time will soon be required, try to introduce it gradually by feeding your dog one hour later, or earlier, as the case may be, until the new time is reached.
• Make sure that both food and water dish are clean at each serving; bacterial cultures from food traces can be harmful.
• The temperature of food and water is important.

The Proper Diet

Food taken directly from either the refrigerator or the stove is too extreme; try to serve it at body temperature. Water that is too cold can also injure internal organs, particularly in the summer when a dog often consumes too much, too fast.

• Once your dog is fully grown and habitually empties its bowl and licks it clean, you can be pretty sure that your dietary proportions are accurate. You can experiment with gradual increases to see if they, too, are licked clean. If not, your dog is sending you a clear message. However, dogs are not always as good a judge as you, your eyesight, and your experience are.

• Once its weight is stabilized, you have the best gauge for determining what brand of food to buy or what type of personalized diet to continue until it reaches old age.

• Occasionally, your chow may greedily bolt large, unchewed portions of especially delectable morsels. Normally its gastric juices can handle it. On occasion, however, the stomach may not be able to do its job, and the dog will vomit. Often it will then proceed to lap up this unappetizing, semisolid mess. Try to maintain your composure and regard it as normal. And, of course, hope that it occurs only occasionally.

Understanding Chow Chows

This chapter is based on a very simple assumption: understanding your dog requires knowing something about the origin of dogs in general and of chow chows in particular. In other words, if you understand where in the animal kingdom your dog comes from, you will have a clearer sense of the origin of its behavioral and thinking patterns.

I hope, therefore, that if you know a little bit about your dog's origins, you will understand why, for example, your chow has its own way of "pointing." To you it may seem characteristic of it alone, and it is special; yet, given the opportunity, most chows will invariably "point" in the same way.

Two other means of understanding your chow chow are readily available to you. First, dogs have an obvious means of helping you to understand them — a language whose vocabulary and signals you need to know something about. Second, specific standards have been established for the breed. Although they originate in physical and external description, they, too, help you understand more about your dog.

History of Dogs

The earliest history of the dog is shrouded in mystery. But the evidence that dogs have always accompanied mankind stretches back to the cave drawings of the Old Stone Age, or Paleolithic period, that ended anywhere from 40,000 to 10,000 years ago. This is also the period of the emergence of *Homo sapiens*, of mankind as we know it today. Hunting scenes in the fascinating cave drawings of southern France and northern Spain created during this period clearly show men and dogs working together. Later archeological evidence shows the dog as decoration on figurines and implements. Archeological digs have also unearthed fossil bones and teeth of wild dogs and their possible ancestors: wolves, jackals, coyotes, and foxes.

Theories abound from these scraps of evidence, but none is conclusive. What can be established about these potential canine ancestors is a similar configuration of teeth. Most theorists believe the wolf is most likely the immediate ancestor, not only because of the configuration of its teeth but also because of the similarity of its blood protein. It is equally true, however, that skulls from Spitz-like dogs have been found in digs among the pillar-dwelling peoples along the Baltic Sea. It is believed that these domesticated dogs descended from jackals, or the wild dogs of Europe.

Much of this evidence is included in the theory put forth 25 years ago by Dr. Reginald H. Smythe. In his book, *The Mind of the Dog*, he divides the prehistoric ancestors of modern dogs into two classifications: "long headed" and "short faced."

Originating in the wolf, the long headed classification breaks down into two groups: one with the modified wolf-like characteristic found in latter-day breeds like the chow chow and the Siberian husky; the other with the truer wolf-like characteristics recognizable in the German Shepherd.

The short faced classification may actually have been a mutation of the long headed type. Since they have shorter faces and jaws as well as more rounded heads, they are closely linked with the jackal, which also has a short muzzle and a domed head. This classification also breaks down into two groups. The larger version is represented by Newfoundlands, Saint Bernards, and Mastiffs; the shorter version, by Spaniels, Pekingeses, and Pugs.

Dr. Smythe further believes that different temperaments followed from these differences in body structure. Because of their closer conformity to the wolf pattern, the long heads traveled in packs, developed a strong pack loyalty, were vigilantly protective of their territory, and survived as inveterate hunters. The short faces, on the other hand, rarely traveled in packs, existed more as companion animals, and came to depend on a master to provide them with food—witness their jaws, which are designed less for killing prey than for crunching it.

These two distinct temperamental types may also go a long way toward explaining why and how dogs are so loyal. The famous researcher of animal

Understanding Chow Chows

behavior, Konrad Lorenz, explores this question in *Man Meets Dog*. He believes that these characteristics exist for two separate reasons. One, though less significant, component of fidelity has to do with factors linking a wild puppy to its mother. These ties last a lifetime. With the domesticated dog, they become translated into a kind of life-long dependence on the human master.

The other source of loyalty takes root in the dog's sense of the pack. This works not only to make the dog's affections constant to its leader but also to instill its fidelity to and within the pack. Lorenz divides dogs into groups that owe more either to the wolf or to the jackal as the predominant ancestor. But the result would be substantially the same when expressed in terms of the long headed and the short faced theory. The former accepts its master as a colleague. Its sense of allegiance is much greater than that of the latter. Furthermore, it is less able to transfer its sense of a bond to someone else.

Lorenz tells a wonderful story about how he had planned to surprise his wife with a birthday present of a chow chow bitch. He purchased the puppy, who was just under six months old, about a week before the actual anniversary and asked his cousin to keep her during the interim. To Lorenz's amazement, that was enough time for the dog to choose the cousin as her rightful owner. Although the cousin rarely visited the Lorenz family, the dog always gravitated to her when she did come. The dog did eventually become quite affectionate with her new mistress. But Lorenz is convinced that this fidelity and love would have been greater had he not sidetracked the process by taking the puppy from the breeding kennel to his cousin's.

This anecdote may help to explain both why the chow chow plays a prominent role in Lorenz's book *King Solomon's Ring* and why Lorenz later in his life bred chow chows.

In which category do you think Lorenz put the chow? The wolf category is correct. Lorenz considers chow chows to be a clear example of a breed whose ancestors were more wolf than jackal. Such dogs invariably choose a master for life at the age of five to six months because this is the age when the influence of the wolf-pack leader would first have begun to make itself felt. In other words, the chow is a dog of the long headed, not the short faced, type.

The Chow Chow's Background

Specifying exactly when chow chows first appeared on the scene is difficult because of a nasty habit common to early Chinese emperors. Since they systematically destroyed whatever cultural examples survived from the previous dynasty, we have only a few early examples of the breed. One is a stylized figurine, currently in the Berlin Museum, from the Han Dynasty (207 B.C. to 220 A.D.), the period from which many date the beginning of modern China. Another example is in a painting from the Imperial eras, generally thought to be over 2,000 years old, depicting an exquisitely groomed dark red dog lying under a table in a well-appointed room. There are also statues of Fu dogs, which look remarkably like chows, that are estimated to be over 3,000 years old.

These artifacts, however, are only latter-day pieces of evidence. Most scholars agree that the breed is one of the oldest known, although they are not in accord about its origin. Some believe it originated in China with the ancient mastiff of Tibet, the name given to the figurine from the Han Dynasty. Still others believe the chow originated in the area around the Arctic Circle, but, because its blue-black tongue is unique, it must have entered China separately. It is thought to have been the ancestor of breeds such as the Samoyed, Norwegian Elkhound, Keeshond, and Pomeranian — although none of these beeeds has its colored tongue. (In the entire animal world, by the way, only certain breeds of bears have a similarly colored tongue.) The compromise view considers the chow chow a crossing of the Samoyed with the Mastiff.

Many people still wonder where the name

Understanding Chow Chows

"chow chow" comes from. Reverend White's description, quoted in the "Foreword," refers to the "*Chinese* breed from *Canton* such as are fattened in that country for the purpose of being eaten." Dog meat has been highly regarded in China for centuries. As recently as 1915, the public buying and selling of the meat from chows was forbidden under Chinese law. Some people even argue that the word *chou* or *chow* was a slang term for "edible" because of the Mandarin Chinese verb *ch'ao,* "to stir," to "fry," or "to cook." Dictionaries, however, generally say that the Cantonese word *kau* or *kao* and the Mandarin *kou* mean "dog." Canton is the city and area with which the breed has most been associated throughout its history. The Chinese themselves have a wide range of designations, which run the gamut from "black-tongue" or "black-mouthed dog" to "wolf dog" and "bear dog."

There is, however, a more plausible theory to explain the origin of the breed's name. The cargo masters of the East India Company, who were involved in the China trade during the late 18th century, had a general term for listing the variety of items they brought back on their bills of lading — "chow chow." The place where they stored these items on their clipper ships was called the "chow chow" hold. In the same location where knick-knacks and bric-a-brac, such as ivory or porcelain figurines, and miscellaneous items were stored, so too were these exotic-looking dogs. Since the first of these dogs to reach England were imported on those ships, the breed gradually acquired the name of the place in which the dogs were kept during their journey to England.

The very early history of the chow centers on its ability to serve its owners. Furthermore, it demonstrates the breed's potential for wreaking havoc with the AKC's current neat categories of sport, hound, and working dogs. Chinese annals record the chow's superior ability to scent, point, and retrieve. They also document its speed and stamina in sled-pulling and sheep- or stock-herding. One extraordinary piece of evidence records that one of the first T'ang emperors in the early 7th century A.D.

maintained a kennel of 2500 couples of chow-type "hounds." This was surely one of the most extravagant kennels in history!

More modern examples of the respect the Chinese have for the chow involve religious sources. In some of the more remote mountainous regions, Buddhist priests still prize the dog, breeding it for its original hunting and protective purposes. And in some temples, the dark or blue chow is regarded as sacred; monks care for them with veneration.

On the other hand, few — if any — of those who first brought the chow chow to England appreciated these qualities. Its value to them was more because of its exotic appearance. In 1820, a newspaper account of the bizarre wild animals imported from China, Japan, and India alluded to a widely admired black-tongued animal with a thick red coat. The London Zoological Garden had a chow it described as "the wild dog" of China. Steady importation of chows into England began in the 1880s, although Queen Victoria received one around 1865. A story, probably spurious, has it that the Queen was so attached to her chow puppy that several ladies-in-waiting hit upon a plan to please her. They hired a dressmaker to design and sew up a stuffed toy to look like her chow puppy. They then presented it to her so that she could cuddle and fondle it more easily and, to their way of thinking, more sanitarily than her puppy.

The 1880s marked the beginning of widespread interest in and acceptance of the breed in England. Diplomats and travelers returning to England brought chows back with them. Also, a particularly fine black chow was part of the Crystal Palace Exhibition in 1880. The English Kennel Club first recorded a chow in 1894; the English Chow Chow Club was established a year later, as was the first standard for the breed.

During this decade the first chow chow was shown in the United States at the Westminster Kennel Club show in 1890. It took third prize in the Miscellaneous Class. By 1906, a chow had won the Best of Breed at Westminster, and the breed rapidly increased in popularity in America. Although interest peaked in the late twenties and early thirties, people are beginning to return to the breed. They do so now more from esteem for its canine qualities than for its function as a household ornament.

This brief survey makes an important point for people considering owning a chow chow. Because of the breed's original purposes and uses, it remains a hefty dog committed to outdoor activity. Its strength, size, power, and instinct for faithful work should all be considered in relation to its place in your home and routine.

Communicating With Your Chow Chow

To make sure you are communicating with your chow, you need to understand the signals your dog sends you. Picking up on them depends on how well your senses are attuned to its signals; these signals, too, are heavily dependent on the dog's senses. Since communication should be two-way, it is a good idea to know not only what signals your dog is sending you, but also what signals you are sending your dog.

Hearing

Your dog's bark tells you a great deal about what it's feeling at that moment. There is a different pitch to a happy dog's bark; in time you will be able to distinguish it from its angry bark. Its growl, howl, whine, whimper, and yelp signal emotions ranging from fear and upset to longing and urgency to excitement. If you watch your dog grow from puppyhood to maturity, you may notice variations in these vocal expressions, but the emotional basis for them will always be the same.

A dog's sense of hearing is extremely acute. Next to its sense of smell, a dog's hearing is its most finely tuned sense. It hears high-pitched and distant sounds much better than you do. Only a few musicians can rival a dog's perception of sound. Yet, the most beautiful sound to your dog's ear will always be your voice.

Sight

Closely related to your dog's vocal expressions is your dog's body language. The position of the tail is one of your surest clues about the dog's emotional state. An erect tail means excitement, although it can easily become aggressive excitement. A wagging tail, with variation in speed, tells you how happy your dog is. A lowered tail usually means either contentment or indifference. Finally, a tail tucked between its legs means your dog is afraid — either of punishment from you or of another dog.

Your chow's body language will be most evident when it meets another dog. During this encounter gender makes a difference. Generally, a male dog will be the aggressor only against another male; this is also usually true of females. In such situations, each dog approaches the other with a stiff-legged, frontal stance, tail erect. Then they make a series of lunges with a retreat for regrouping to make a better lunge. Finally, the dog acknowledging defeat sinks into a cringing, crouching position. The encounter ends with the yelping flight of the loser with its tail between its legs, or with the conquered dog rolling onto its back and exposing its defenseless throat to the victor. If the two dogs are male and female, their ritual begins with cordially erect, wagging tails, followed by the mating dance with its complicated series of undulating movements that first invite and reject the male's advances, and finally signal the female's complaisant acceptance.

Dogs also use body language to warn you to back off. These signals are somewhat similar to those it sends other dogs. Watch for the stiff-legged, frontal stance; the erect tail; the flattened, laid-back ears; the teeth bared with lips drawn back; the hackles and neck fur raised to make you think it is larger than it is; the silent, purposeful track; the forward crouch, its springing position; growling and snarling, often with snapping or biting, from the

Understanding Chow Chows

sitting or standing position; and, finally, the spring — usually for the throat.

If you ever find yourself the victim of a springing dog, tell yourself to freeze, not to struggle. Freezing is your best defense because it sends the dog the signal that it has pinned or captured you; it is the victor.

I offer a word of caution if, while walking your chow on a lead, you meet a dog that wants to fight. If your dog is trained properly, you can avoid a fight with verbal commands. If you realize, however, that a fight is inevitable, both dogs will fare better with their leads removed. They will have more room to fight, to withdraw, and to determine which is dominant. Despite the horrendous and frightening noises, death is not the object. Furthermore, your intervention in the fight may do more harm than good — not only to your dog but also to yourself. Neither dog wants to lose face with its owner nearby. Your attempt to yank the hind legs apart or to douse them with cold water will probably not work. Let them settle it themselves.

As for dogs' ability to see, the fact is that vision is one of a dog's less-developed senses.

Touch

A chow tells you a lot through touch. The messages all concern affection — the casual nuzzle, the strategic placement of a paw, or the desperate curling up at the foot of your bed on a cold winter's night.

You also tell your pet a great deal by how and when you touch it. Mostly, you give reassurance — that you still love it; that you want to make sure it has not been hurt or become ill; or that you want to calm it after a frightening experience. And, of course, the time when your pet will need your reassurance most is that dreaded moment when it has to be put to sleep. Stroking it gently with as much calm as you can muster resonating in your voice may even help *you* get through that wrenching experience.

Dogs prefer to be stroked rather than patted. Of course, you will soon learn what area your chow prefers you to scratch. Because it interprets your strokes as soothing and affectionate, your dog's response will be more positively cooperative. Patting is often interpreted as superficial and may make your dog nervous.

When approaching a strange dog, offer it the back of your hand before trying to touch it. This gives the dog your scent, its best means for knowing and remembering you.

Smell

A much greater area of a dog's brain is devoted to reading signals from its nose than is that of a human. A dog's nostril has about 25 times more surface area for receiving data than does a human nostril. This may explain why your grungy sneakers or dirty socks are some of your dog's sources of greatest consolation. When you return home and find these items strewn all over the house, you may become angry. Remember, though, that your dog has just offered you a sincere gesture of affection.

Dogs determine friend and enemy alike, whether human or animal, by scent. They deposit their urine, even to the point of some males meting it out in numerous, small doses, so other dogs will know that this particular turf has already been staked out. All that sniffing to determine the perfect spot may prolong your walk, but it is essential to the dog's status in its community. And, amazing as it may seem, a mother dog can distinguish any of her litter from all the others by scent.

One other significant line of communication is a dog's ability to smell emotions. Although you don't realize you give off a scent of fear, hate, violence, acceptance, or love, your dog recognizes your emotions immediately — as well as those of potential friends or enemies. How dogs interpret this knowledge is an important component of their behavioral patterns. Thus, if you are ever threatened by a dog, appearing calm and confident may help mask your fear. At the very least, you will send the dog a mixed message: a scent of fear along with

Understanding Chow Chows

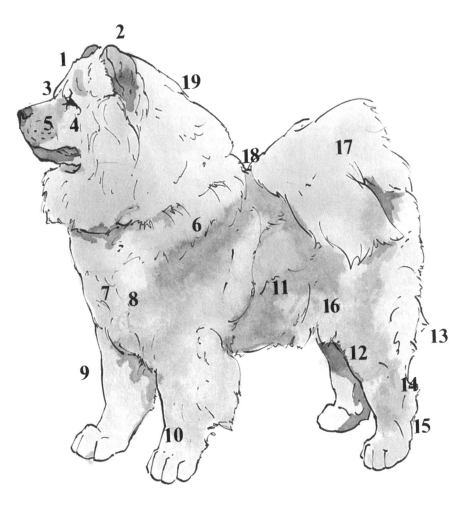

Knowing the parts of a chow will help you understand AKC standards.

1. Skull	8. Brisket	15. Rear pastern
2. Ears	9. Forequarters	16. Loin
3. Stop	10. Front pastern	17. Tail
4. Cheek	11. Rib cage	18. Withers
5. Muzzle	12. Stifle	19. Neckline
6. Shoulder	13. Hindquarters	
7. Chest	14. Hock	

a message of strength through your bearing. The latter may serve you well.

Taste

Your dog loves to lick you. Licking is innate to dogs, whether it be for sociability, self-grooming, or as a way for a mother dog to comfort and clean her pups. You should tolerate a few welcoming licks because it is your dog's most direct means of communicating love and affection. But for sanitary reasons, don't encourage your chow to lick you all over.

A final note: any change in your dog's finely tuned communication signals is another clear signal in itself. One of your first clues to illness or accident will be something unusual about the way these languages are being used. If what you have grown to expect to be customarily or habitually present is absent, then chances are something is not quite right with your dog.

Understanding the Standards for Chow Chows

A final component in your understanding of your chow chow is knowing something about the official breed standards established by the AKC in 1941. You can consult them for the exact wording; here are some general guidelines. Even if you have no intention of ever showing your chow, it is interesting to know about the external, physical standard a judge might apply to your dog.

A lot of attention is given to a chow's head. In proportion to the dog's body, it should be broad and large, with a fairly flat skull, a moderate stop (the gradation between the skull and muzzle located between the eyes), and a muzzle squared off and boxlike, so that its length, width, and depth are roughly equal. The area underneath the eyes should be filled out well, and the muzzle should not be sharply pointed or tapered, as is the Alaskan

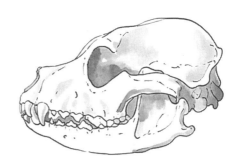

The chow chow's skull should be broad and flat with a moderate stop. Note, too, the scissors bite; the teeth should not be overshot or undershot.

Malamute's. The leonine ruff is the head's crowning glory because it heightens the beauty of both head and body. The visible part of the eye should be almond-shaped, dark, and set deeply into the dog's head, not protruding. A chow's ears should be small and widely set, with slightly rounded tips that the dog carries up and tilted forward. The nose is to be broad and black; the tongue, of course, is to be blue-black. Pigmentation within puppies varies; all chow puppies are born with a nose that is lighter than black and a pink tongue. Do not worry about how fast the changes occur: strongly pigmented dogs will change at three weeks, whereas others may not until they reach ten months. A chow should have a scissors bite; as with most breeds, its jaws are not to be overshot or undershot.

The body of a chow should be balanced and, like the muzzle, square. The more rectangular the body — so that the length from shoulders to rump is longer than the dog's height — the less it meets the standard. The straight shoulders should slope slightly. A long neck is undesirable; it should be strong and full. The chest should never be narrow, but rather broad and deep; it should come down approximately to the middle of the dog's elbows. The chow's topline should be level, encompassing

Understanding Chow Chows

The chow chow's unique blue-black tongue. The mouth tissue should be almost all black, too.

A chow sports a double coat: the topcoat is thick, dense, straight, and, if possible, long; the undercoat, soft and woolly. Because the texture is harsh, the coat does not lie flat on the dog's body. It should also have a sheen, but its color should be solid, with lighter shading permissible on the ruff, tail, and breechings. Both the color and size, by the way, are left unspecified, although the standard does specify that the coat be of "untouched naturalness." Although you should brush it regularly, never cut, trim, pluck, or otherwise neaten the chow's coat.

a strong, straight back, ribs set close together, and broad, powerful loins. The tail, also finely displayed, is high-set and carried close to the back so there is no space between it and its resting position on the dog's spine. When the dog moves, however, the tail will naturally move up. Some chows have a little kink or curl at the tail's end; however, as long as it is carried correctly, this is not a negative feature.

Since the legs, too, affect the sense of balance, you want them to look "cobby" (like a short-legged, stocky horse) but well-proportioned. The forelegs are straight and heavy-boned, as are the hind legs — but these present a problem. The hocks, which correspond to our ankles, should be straight, too, not a standard most breeds must meet. Straight hocks may be an evolutionary response to the chow's need, early in its history, to move nimbly through deep snow. The result is a rarity among dogs' gaits: the chow's is stilted, with a slight roll and with short, choppy rear steps. The feet are to be round and catlike.

Fine specimens of the breed. Although AKC standards do not specify size or weight for chows, this illustration indicates the relative size of the male and female chow.

Finally, the dog's coat is rhapsodically described as a "masterpiece of beauty and dignity" and its expression is called "essentially dignified, lordly, scowling, discerning, sober, and snobbish— one of independence." The chow's scowl results from the wrinkling of the loose skin on the dog's forehead and around its eyes. Most admirers of chows hold its scowling standoffishness in high esteem. It is the chow's final, endearing touch.

Caring for Your Chow Chow

Bringing Your Puppy Home

Since this chapter discusses general care and recommendations appropriate throughout your dog's life, let's begin with bringing your puppy home.

As in the development of a child, these early weeks and months are crucial to the dog's later behavior. If your puppy is eight weeks or more, it has just completed the imprinting phase and is now in the socialization phase. It relates to its littermates and to humans through periods during which it plays and becomes serious. It is testing the limits of its own potential as well as the limits you are setting. Because it is anxious to learn and to please, its socialization depends a great deal on the guidelines you provide. By five to six months, it is ready to pledge its allegiance to you. You must rise to the occasion. Before it reaches maturity, however, it will go through the equivalent of the adolescent rebellion phase. It will continually test your will to remain dominant. Thus, your chow's socialization requires thought and perseverance.

Socialization of Your Chow Chow

Regardless of your puppy's age when you bring it home, it will take some time to get over its loneliness and to adapt to its new surroundings. Let it sniff to its heart's content, show it where you keep its food and water dishes, and, when it shows signs of tiring, put it into its new bed. If it is paper trained, try to get it to that location as soon as you see that it needs to go. Otherwise, take it outside as soon as necessary. Also, try to bring your new puppy home during a period when you will not have to leave it alone for the first several days. During this time, your puppy may feel abandoned. This sense of abandonment may lead to household destruction as a means of consolation and retaliation.

Proper diet and sleep are important during the puppy's first weeks with you. To avoid digestive upset, continue feeding the same food used by the breeder. Also, introduce any necessary changes gradually. Overlapping the breeder's diet and your own, with a corresponding reduction in portions, is a good way to shift to your preferred diet. Try to adapt to the puppy's sleep patterns and interfere as little as possible with them. This may require extra effort from your children. Also, caution them not to disturb the dog while it is eating.

Although I will discuss specific training techniques in the last chapter, your puppy must learn several things during its first weeks with you: to come when you call its name, to become housebroken, not to beg for food, to behave when left alone, and to begin its collar and leash training.

Finally, we need to raise one additional point about socializing a chow chow. Some people think the breed is unfriendly, standoffish, temperamental, difficult to handle, aggressive toward other dogs and people, and unreliable. Although there may be some truth to these accusations, remember that as an owner, you exert a lot of control over how people perceive your dog and how it represents the breed.

From the day it becomes part of your household, you need to begin socializing your chow. If it is from your own litter, pick it up even before its eyes open; if you get the puppy from a breeder, pick it up frequently, cuddle it warmly, pet it, and speak to it gently. Encourage your children and others to become involved in the socialization process. Introduce new areas for it to adapt to — your car, the park, a schoolyard, busy sidewalks — always making sure that your firm, enthusiastic voice is there to comfort and urge it forward into the new and unfamiliar. Furthermore, introduce your young dog to other puppies and dogs early on. Encourage it to play with them. Also, be sure you chase, romp, and play with it often. If the situation becomes too rough, calm your puppy gradually, soothing it, picking it up, and giving it lots of hugs. Your chow will then readily demonstrate its goodwill to others, its stability, and its dependability. It will be a credit to both you and the breed.

Basic Grooming

The Coat

As the breed standard makes clear, the chow's coat is one of its most important attributes. People unfamiliar with the breed, however, take one look at its coat and assume keeping it well groomed is extremely time-consuming. Actually, it takes no more than five minutes a day — or one extended period a week — to groom a chow. This is also true for your puppy. Begin by making grooming part of its daily routine. Choose any position you like; however, the job is often easier for you — and less boring and tiring for the dog — if you accustom it to lying down. Also, it is easier to brush difficult to reach areas, such as its stomach and the backs of its legs, when it is lying down.

The direction of the arrows indicates proper grooming of the chow chow's coat. This three-quarter perspective is also the best angle for photographing your chow chow.

Start with the body, move on to the hips and breeching, and then brush the ruff and shoulders. Once you have turned the dog over and repeated this order, you are ready to get it up and brush its head and tail. At the end of the session, brush the coat forward, against the lay of the hair, toward the head. You may want to use a comb, lifting it through the coat, and a soft brush to finish the job. Be careful with the area around the ears, where the hair is fine and can mat easily.

Proper brushing requires parting the coat evenly at small intervals and brushing thoroughly from the part out to the ends of the hair. When combing the soft, woolly undercoat, do not comb it out entirely. When it is ready to come out, as it will be during the summer, it will do so naturally. Although puppies are often best groomed only with a comb, do not overuse it on a mature dog. If you are showing your chow, you may occasionally want to purchase a coat conditioner to heighten its sheen.

The Eyes and Ears

Your chow's ears require special attention. If there is any problem you will soon find out. Dogs announce an ear problem by incessant head shaking, pawing, scratching, or other unusual behavior.

I will discuss specific ear problems in the chapter on health care; however, as part of your regular grooming routine, examine your dog's ears. Your veterinarian or a pet supply shop can give you liquid products to apply to the ears. Make sure you understand the directions and follow them carefully. After you pour the cleaner into the outer ear and work it around for a minute, your chow will be in a frenzy of excitement and only too happy to shake out the excess liquid and, with it, the dissolved earwax. Avoid probing the ear with a cotton swab unless your veterinarian or other expert has shown you how to do it. Because the ears are so vital to your dog, they need careful, correct attention.

Camaraderie is also a hallmark of the breed when it is expressed toward one of its own (above) or toward other pets in the family (below).

Caring for Your Chow Chow

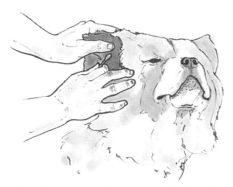

A chow chow's ears need special care, but learn how to use a cotton swab before attempting to clean your dog's ears. Do not probe inside the ear canal!

There are also things to remember in caring for your dog's eyes. Because dogs have a third eyelid, a thin flexible membrane, they do not have to blink, as we do, to remove dirt from the eye. Sometimes, however, specks of dirt are trapped in the gummy discharge that collects in the corners of the eyes during sleep. Remove this gently with a clean, dry cloth. Excessive tearing or blinking and redness around the eyes are problems for your veterinarian.

Some chows are susceptible to a problem known as an inverted eyelid. This occurs when the tiny hairs around the rim of the lower eyelid grow in toward the surface of the eye and scratch the eyeball. Because this condition can be both painful and harmful, it requires surgery by a veterinarian to correct it.

Excellent specimens of chow chows. Note that there is no standard color designated for the breed, but the blue color of the tongue is unique.

The mechanism of your dog's eyes resembles a camera. Be sure to keep the eyes clean.

The Toenails and Pads

As you groom your chow, don't forget its toenails. If your chow's nails grow too long, you may find your floors, furniture, and even your children scratched unnecessarily. Normal exercise may wear down the nails enough so that you will not have to trim them. If you do have to, purchase a good pair of toenail clippers and have your veterinarian or an experienced dog handler show you how to use them. If you cut too close to the nerve endings and blood vessels that run through each nail, you will cause your dog unnecessary pain and bleeding.

Also check your dog's pads for pebbles, thorns, or small objects that might get stuck between them. Use tweezers when necessary and relieve the pain with a soothing compress of isopropyl alcohol. In winter the salt used to melt ice and snow contains caustic material that can eat away at a dog's pads and leave an open, painful spot. You can prevent this by washing the paws with warm water right after bringing the dog in from the outside. Since the chow loves snow, it may need your foresight in this matter. In any case, consult your veterinarian if there is swelling or inflammation.

Caring for Your Chow Chow

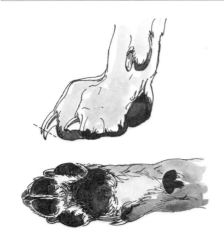

Clip your chow chow's nails at an angle. Be certain not to cut into the quick.

The guillotine nail clipper, one of several types that are available, performs the job well.

Chows are often rather skittish about having their nails trimmed or their feet attended to. Therefore, begin sensitizing your dog to this activity while it is still a puppy. Since the only trimming the AKC Standard permits is that of the long guard hairs on the feet — so that they are round, compact, and catlike — puppyhood is a good time to begin this, too.

Teeth

Before you finish grooming your chow, be sure to examine its teeth briefly. Though bad breath will often tell you all you need to know, it is easy enough to get your dog accustomed to this kind of examination as a puppy. Grip its upper jaw with one hand and open its mouth by pulling the lower jaw down with the other hand. If tartar is beginning to build up, start to increase hard foods, commercial dog biscuits, or rawhide bones in its diet and play routine. If the tartar has yet to harden, swab the teeth with a toothbrush or with cotton balls soaked with lemon juice or with a mixture of half milk and half hydrogen peroxide. On the other hand, if the tartar has hardened, take the dog to your veterinarian to have it removed.

Bathing

If you groom your dog carefully and regularly, you will not need to bathe it often — perhaps once or twice a year. But wait until it is mature; avoid bathing a puppy. Frequent baths diminish your dog's ability to withstand the effects of wind and weather because they reduce the natural fats and oils in its skin and coat. There are times, however, when a bath is a good idea. Salt water is not good for your dog's coat, so bathe it after prolonged periods of exposure to salt. A bath is also good at the end of the summer, or after whelping, when your bitch is going out of coat. Never bathe a bitch during pregnancy. Of course, bathing is also necessary after your dog has been playing in mud or manure — a favorite though highly revolting pastime.

Try to make your dog's bath, especially its first one, as pleasant as possible. Few dogs like baths; most regard them as trials that they, at best, tolerate.

Caring for Your Chow Chow

Choose a place that is convenient for you and where you can wear as few clothes as possible — a bathtub or, in summer, your backyard.

First, comb and brush the dog, then put a few drops of mineral oil in the eyes to protect them against the soap. Use a dog shampoo to help restore some of the natural fats and oils to the coat. Since fats and oils will be lost anyway, the coat may lose its beautiful sheen for several days. After lathering the dog, work the shampoo into the coat and spray warm — not hot — water as a rinse. Because a dog can get chilled quickly, even on a warm day, have a thick towel ready to wrap it up in before it starts shaking water everywhere.

When neither you nor your dog is up to a bath, use a warm, damp towel to clean it. Soak a towel in a little bit of shampoo and some water and rub it briskly over the coat, drying thoroughly — when finished.

Daily Life With Your Chow Chow

Living with Children

Snapshots of children cavorting in a field with a puppy or tussling with one on the playroom floor are often among a family's treasured remembrances. But children can also be careless and unintentionally cruel to puppies and dogs. They may pull on their ears, tails, and coats, or play games in which they keep the dog prisoner in a closet or tied to a tree. Hence, you need to explain to children, whatever their ages, the rudiments of communicating with dogs and interpreting the dog's signals. Teach young children never to try to play with the puppy when it is eating or sleeping.

Certainly, you should encourage your children to play with your chow; however, especially when both are young, supervise the play periods closely. Because they have a lot of excess energy, children are wonderful exercisers of puppies. Again, though, make sure they stop before the puppy becomes too tired. An excellent means of bringing the two to-gether is to let your children share in the responsibility of caring for the dog. In this way, the puppy will become friends with your children more rapidly. Taking on these responsibilities will boost your children's self-esteem and teach them to be reliable pet owners in the future. Gradually increase your children's participation in caring for your dog. Start by putting them in charge of the water dish, then let them put down and clean up the food dish. Later, as their mutual trust and friendship increase, let them brush the puppy and walk it on a lead. Use your discretion about leaving children and dog alone; once you achieve mutual respect, it is usually quite safe.

One dangerous aspect of developing mutual trust and respect is that your children may automatically assume that all dogs will behave with them exactly as does your chow. Tell them emphatically that this is not so. Teach them not to approach strange dogs and not to pet them. Rather, tell them to let the dog approach them while they, without making any startling movements, talk calmly to the dog and extend the backs of their hands for it to sniff and get their scent.

Living with a New Baby

Just as you may expect some rivalry for your attention, once a new baby arrives, from your older children, so you may expect your dog to feel left out and start competing for your affection. Gradually give your dog opportunities to meet and sniff the newborn while you talk to the dog calmly and reassuringly. Also, make an effort to spread your love and affection around equally.

Try to keep your dog from licking the infant. If it does, merely wash the area afterward. Dogs that are properly wormed, vaccinated, and cared for rarely carry germs harmful to a baby. Nevertheless, just to be safe, have your chow examined by your veterinarian several weeks before the baby is due. Although you will have other things on your mind at that time, you will welcome the knowledge that your dog is well.

Caring for Your Chow Chow

Living with Other Pets

It's usually easy to introduce a puppy into a household with other pets. If the other pet is a cat or kitten, the two will generally become friends by playing together. In my experience, "fighting like cats and dogs" is something that happens only when neighbors' pets are involved. Our cats and dogs have gotten along beautifully. Even though we were always ready to separate them, it was unnecessary. Birds, mice, guinea pigs, or hamsters, however, are fair game for a chow, so keep them in their cages whenever your dog is around.

Living with Another Dog

You should be able to predict that introducing a second dog into your household will present some problems. You can understand that this situation may disturb the first dog's sense of loyalty to you. If both are mature dogs, the situation is more difficult than if one is a puppy. Your natural inclination to help the underdog (or, in this case, the "underpuppy") needs to be restrained. Just as a mature dog and a puppy will usually determine which will dominate, so two puppies will also usually determine this themselves. As they vie for rank and your loving attention, however, your evenhandedness must always be evident.

Be absolutely impartial when dealing with such daily routines as feeding, sleeping arrangements, taking walks, handing out and playing with toys, and dispensing treats. Each of these situations requires special purchases, which should be done before you introduce the second dog. Feed both dogs simultaneously but from different dishes; one water dish, however, is enough. If one is a puppy, it will have to eat more often than the older dog. To prevent strife in this situation, give the older dog a small portion of the puppy's food. This will help minimize the older dog's envy over the "better" smell of the puppy's food. Of course, you must then reduce the amount of food you give the older dog at its regular feedings.

You will need new equipment, too. Buy a new bed for the second dog and place it at some distance from the first dog's bed. Eventually, you may be able to bring them closer; they may even like the companionship later on. You will also need another lead so that you can walk both dogs together. Remember that puppies need more frequent walks—after each meal. Walk with one dog on your right and the other on your left. Although they will try to confuse the pattern, they will get used to it after some tangles and tugging. Be sure the new toys are appropriate for the puppy, and do not allow either dog to play with the other's toys. Play with them individually at first, and introduce group play only when their relationship is well established. Finally, make sure treats are appropriately sized, but different enough so that the dogs will not confuse the smells. Then each dog will know which treat it "deserves."

No matter how judicious you are, though, the adjustment will not be without incident. In three to six weeks, however, the two dogs will have determined the balance of power. The less you interfere, having taken the steps advised above, the better—and faster—this will be accomplished. Sometimes the play will get rough. Separate them only if the shrill, painful yelps become too prolonged or too frequent.

Your role will be a more active one if your second dog is of the same sex as the first. The older dog is quite likely to feel embattled, since a chow's attachment to its owner is usually a fiercely loyal one. This situation will probably resolve itself eventually, but you must be sure to treat both dogs with complete fairness.

Living with an Older Dog

Once your dog is six years old, it should have a general physical examination every six months. Remember, the better care you give your young dog, the fewer problems your older dog will have. Aging is accelerated when sickness and injuries are

Caring for Your Chow Chow

neglected early in a dog's life. You will probably find that your chow chow's tolerance for changes in its daily routine decreases as it ages, and that it is generally less active. Pay special attention to your dog's muscle tone, stiffening of the joints, and its diet. As a matter of fact, many of the things you would consider for yourself as you age are equally applicable to your dog. The following chart gives you an idea of how your chow ages in comparison to the human aging process:

dog	human	dog	human
6 months	10 years	9 years	52 years
1 year	15 years	10 years	56 years
2 years	24 years	11 years	60 years
3 years	28 years	12 years	64 years
4 years	32 years	13 years	68 years
5 years	36 years	14 years	72 years
6 years	40 years	15 years	76 years
7 years	44 years	16 years	80 years
8 years	48 years	21 years	100 years

Lifting and Carrying a Dog

You can harm your puppy or grown dog by improper handling. Instead of picking a puppy up by the scruff of the neck, put one arm around its chest and the other around its back legs. Hold your arms close to the dog's chest so that you will not drop it if it starts to squirm. This is also the best way to carry a grown dog. If your dog is injured, avoid putting pressure on the wound. Lay the dog on its side and carry it in a blanket or on a stretcher.

Tattooing

Before making vacation plans for your chow, consider protecting your dog with a harmless tattoo that will insure its identification. An amazing number of stolen and lost dogs are returned to their owners through tattoo identification. Dogs are usually tattooed in the groin area or on the inside of the ear. Use either the dog's AKC registration number or your Social Security number. Ask your veterinarian about this procedure. Registration centers will record your dog's number and, in an emergency, help you locate it. Even if you do not plan to travel extensively, tattooing your dog will give you peace of mind.

Photographing

Most of the pictures you take of your chow will be with family members — children cuddling with a puppy or a dog's alert response to a clever trick. Occasionally, however, you may want to include your chow in a family portrait or take a rather formal portrait of it alone. Because profile shots tend to emphasize unflatteringly its length and height, avoid this angle. Instead, aim so that the dog's body is in a three-quarter position, and it is looking at the camera. Now the emphasis will be on its magnificent head and its singular scowl.

Vacationing

Before you plan a vacation, whether for a weekend or for an extended period of time, you must make plans for your chow. For a brief trip, perhaps a neighbor can care for it. Urban areas sometimes have organizations that list house- and pet-sitters; some sitters will even take your dog into their own homes. If this service is available, try to arrange a get-acquainted session before you depart. Once you see how your dog and the sitter interact, you will feel better about entrusting your chow to this "foster parent."

During the first eight months or so of your puppy's life, however, try not to have to leave it — even with someone whom you trust to care for it properly. The paramount issue is not so much the care being given the puppy as it is the successful bonding between the puppy and you. Remember Konrad Lorenz's story about the chow he wanted to present his wife on her birthday. During these crucial months, the more regular the routine you maintain with your chow, the happier your future life together will be.

Caring for Your Chow Chow

One means of maintaining this routine is to take your dog with you on vacation. This may require adjusting your plans. It will certainly require flexibility and foresight. Happily, more and more hotel and motel chains are permitting guests to bring their dogs with them. Obtain a list of them and plan to stay at such places.

There is, obviously, another solution: board your chow at a kennel. Unfortunately, chows feel the same separation anxiety as do children. If your dog is accustomed to a bustling household and you as a steady companion, even the best kennel will not be satisfactory.

Kennel standards, of course, vary a great deal. If you decide to board your dog, get the best possible advice about local, high-quality kennels. Your first choice should be the kennel from which you bought your chow; your second choice might be a kennel recommended by your veterinarian. You might also take the recommendation of a dog lover whom you trust. Do not consider any boarding kennel that neglects to ask you for a vaccination certificate against distemper/hepatitis/leptospirosis, parainfluenza, parvovirus, and rabies. Your assurance that the kennel strictly follows health codes is its insistence upon receiving current vaccination records.

Traveling by Car: If you decide to take your chow with you on vacation, be sure to plan your itinerary and mode of transportation carefully in advance. You also need confidence in your dog's obedience training before you leave. It is essential for your safety and your dog's that your chow respond properly to *lie down, sit,* and *stay.*

Find out in advance — either through a travel agent or by yourself — which hotels and motels will accommodate your dog and what restrictions apply. This is the most important part of your vacation planning, at least as far as your chow is concerned.

Your chow should already be accustomed to travel by car. If you know you will want to take your dog on car trips, start acclimating it while it is still a puppy. If you start early — after eight weeks — you will soon know if your dog can tolerate car

trips. Dogs should occupy only the back seat of a car or the rear area of a station wagon. The front seat is too hazardous. Remember that your dog will be more comfortable if your children let it doze rather than try to play with it.

To increase your dog's comfort in the car, be sure it has some air, but not too much; drafts can cause ear and eye problems. Do not allow your dog to stick its head out the window. Also, rest stops every two hours will allow you to stretch your legs and your dog to walk around and relieve itself.

Unfortunately, many dog owners lose their pets while on vacation because the owners fail to use a lead when stopping to rest. Many dogs are likely to bolt when confused by unfamiliar sounds, smells, and surroundings. Using a lead is a simple precaution — and it can spare you needless heartache. Although it may not make your dog more comfortable, it will make you a happier vacationer.

Water, whether provided at rest stops or from a bottle kept in a cool place, is also a welcome relief for your dog on hot summer days. Ice-cold water, however, can harm your dog's stomach. It's also good to pack some treats or dry food, but not canned food that needs refrigeration. Do not give human treats or scraps from a fast-food stop. Pack the kind of treats your dog is used to, in order to maintain its regular routine.

Finally, ask your veterinarian if he or she advises motion sickness medicine or a mild tranquilizer to be given to your dog several hours before you depart. Be sure you know your dog's reaction to any medication *before* you leave. It is difficult, even for your veterinarian, to predict whether or not your dog will have an adverse reaction to medication. Each dog reacts differently.

Traveling by Train and Airplane: Most railroads require that, because of its size, your chow must travel in a container in the baggage car. Regardless of how long you will spend on the train, find out before purchasing your ticket, what regulations apply to dogs and whether or not you may visit your dog en route.

With airlines, too, it is essential to verify the

arrangements before you purchase tickets. You will need to consider pressurized luggage compartments and the appropriate size container for your dog. The national ASPCA, and perhaps your local office, has a booklet that provides advice about appropriate container sizes. A container that measures $36 \times 22 \times 26$ inches ($91 \times 56 \times 66$ cm) is appropriate, as long as your chow is not larger than 22 inches (56 cm) at the shoulders. Some airlines lend containers, others rent them; a safe bet is to purchase your own. It should have a sliding-door grill for feeding, watering, and ventilation, and a waterproof bottom. Be sure to label it with your delivery and home addresses, and your dog's name. Sometimes hearing its name used, even by a stranger, will reassure a nervous dog. As an added precaution, put all this information in a weatherproof container and attach it to the dog's collar.

Do not feed your chow just before its flight. Rather, feed it something light six hours prior to departure and give it a little water about two hours before the flight. Give it a good walk before turning it over to the attendants, being sure to inform them of your dog's diet and the location of the dry food you have provided.

Traveling Abroad: International travel requires knowledge of numerous quarantine regulations. Australia, England, Holland, Japan, and Sweden are among the countries with such regulations. Check in advance with the consulate of each country you plan to visit. Also, be prepared for changes in these regulations. Countries that will admit your chow also require health and inoculation certificates, and these requirements are rarely uniform. To avoid problems, be sure you understand these requirements before you travel.

Traveling Equipment: As I have already mentioned, you will need your dog's food and water dishes, its customary food and treat, a water bottle, and a lead when you travel. Other helpful articles include a muzzle — required in some areas — your dog's bed or favorite blanket, a brush, and — in summer — a can of anti-flea and lice spray. It's also good to take a folder with all of your chow chow's licenses and inoculation certificates, for use in an emergency.

Depending on how well your dog adapts to car travel and how far you plan to travel, you may need some kind of kenneling container. Many people buy safari cages and always use them on car trips. Some use them even for local trips. These cages prevent your dog from jumping around in the car and provide a safe, comfortable, secure area of its own. They also collapse easily for convenient storage.

Whether or not you choose to buy a container for use on planes depends upon how frequently you fly. The safari type is too open and therefore unacceptable to most airlines. One advantage of buying an airline-type kennel is the opportunity it gives you to accustom your dog to it before you depart.

Finally, wherever you travel, be sure to take a first-aid kit along. A car first-aid kit will probably lack some items you might need for your dog: material and implements for cleaning its ears, petroleum jelly, cotton and cotton swabs, medicated powder, bacitracin-neomycin ointment, gauze bandage, adhesive tape, plastic bandages, boric acid powder, and remedies for constipation and diarrhea — parafin oil and charcoal tablets. Ask your veterinarian what items should be included.

Your veterinarian, by the way, ought to be the final arbiter in all questions about your chow chow's care. The emphasis in this chapter has been on the ordinary kind of care your dog will require. For those of you with female dogs, the next chapter offers some specific pointers. In Sickness and in Health also deals with concerns about care, but those more directly requiring a veterinarian's attention: routine check-ups and the sick dog.

When Your Bitch Is in Heat

If you own a female chow chow, you need to understand its reproductive cycle and the entire breeding regimen. Breeding is a complex issue, and deciding whether or not to breed your bitch is a question not easily resolved. This chapter offers you some guidelines for these concerns.

A Bitch in Estrus

Your female chow will come into heat any time after the sixth month — usually in the tenth month — and definitely before the 18th month. Hence, you need to make some decisions before she comes into heat. It is unadvisable to breed her during her first season. Also, you should understand her estrus (heat) cycle.

Warning signals of approaching heat include general restlessness and skittish sexual play with neighborhood male dogs. When you begin to notice a bloody discharge — for which you can buy a kind of sanitary pad — and swollen genitals, it means that in about nine days, your bitch will accept a male. This period also lasts about nine days, during which the alluring scent she emits becomes even more powerful; it will attract males to your doorstep from miles away. You can get chlorophyll tablets to curb the scent, or your veterinarian can administer hormone shots. Because such shots may eventually upset the dog's hormone balance, most veterinarians do not approve of them.

Your last resort is to confine your bitch during this three-to-four week period. But beware! She is just as likely to travel miles to find an acceptable male as he is to travel miles to track her down. You may not be aware of all the usable exits your house has — until it is too late. Also, when walking your dog during this period, carry her some distance from your house before putting her down. This way the trail she leaves will not lead directly to your yard, and you will not feel as if you are living under siege.

If all these precautions fail, do not despair. You may have heard that a litter of mongrel puppies prevents a bitch from later having a purebred one. This is untrue, and you probably ought to let her have her litter, raise them carefully, and make sure that you find loving, responsible homes for them. In any event, consult your veterinarian as soon as possible after the impregnation. Under certain circumstances, he may recommend administering a mismate shot (of estrogen) or performing a hysterectomy.

Occasionally, about six to ten weeks after estrus, a bitch exhibits signs of false pregnancy. Her actions lead you to believe that she is preparing herself for whelping. Physical signs include swollen teats. In fact, however, she is not pregnant. This condition often disappears within three months. In any case, consult your veterinarian because false pregnancy can be harmful to your bitch. Furthermore, once a bitch has experienced false pregnancy, she is predisposed to the condition; spaying may be the only long-term solution.

Let's not forget that spaying is another alternative for dealing with a bitch in heat. Your veterinarian can offer sound advice for dealing with the question of neutering—whether you own a male or a female dog. Be aware that there is no medical evidence to support the arguments that if you spay you are depriving your female of a necessary experience or that she will be better off if permitted to bear at least one litter. In addition, humane societies and animal care organizations warn us of the enormity of the population explosion problem among dogs. Think carefully about this important question.

To Breed or not to Breed

For many people the answer lies in how involved they want to become, not only in breeding dogs as a hobby or as a business, but also in developing dogs suitable for dog shows. This, in turn, involves knowledge of the standards established by the AKC for chow chows and of how to achieve these standards genetically.

When Your Bitch Is in Heat

A male chow's reproductive organs.
1. Prostrate
2. Rectum
3. Anus
4. Section of pelvic bone
5. Testicle
6. Scrotum
7. Bulb (part of penis)
8. Penis
9. Sheath
10. Vas deferens
11. Bladder

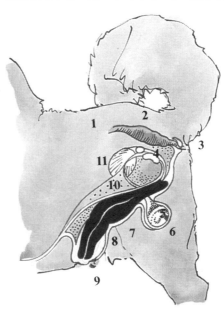

A female chow's reproductive organs.
1. Vulva
2. Anus
3. Rectum
4. Uterus
5. Kidney
6. Ovary
7. Ribs
8. Developing embryo
9. Vagina

When Your Bitch Is in Heat

Do not commit yourself to raising chows for profit or for show until you have considered it seriously, have prior breeding experience, have learned the basic genetic principles of dog breeding, and have a great deal of time to devote to the project. The chows added to the worldwide dog population should be bred by professionals. It is rarely advisable to proceed merely because you think you know of a good stud dog or because your female has inadvertently become pregnant—even by a pedigreed male chow.

If, despite these warnings, you decide to breed your bitch anyway, get to know other interested members of your local chow club and obtain advice from the AKC. Have your veterinarian check your bitch for necessary vaccinations and booster shots; she should also be tested for brucellosis, a disease that causes sterility, and for parasites. Make arrangements with the owner of the stud; a fee is usually involved, or you may have to give the stud's owner the right to choose the pick of the litter. In addition, you will have to take your bitch to the male for the mating. The best time to do so is between the eleventh and thirteenth day after the onset of estrus. A sure sign is a change in the color of the discharge from dark red to a yellowish red. You must keep careful records during the heat periods.

The actual mating is a dazzling but, often, alarming scene. There is a definite sequence of events, in some respects reminiscent of the attack ritual. And many an owner of a bitch, appalled by the sight of the whirling, frenzied ballet, has had to be held back from instinctively interfering. The pair may be locked together in the tie for 10 to 15 minutes, or as long as half an hour. Both can be irreparably harmed if you try to separate them. Let nature take its course.

The Birthday

The puppies will be due between 58 and 63 days after the breeding date. In the meantime, make sure

A whelping box should be large enough to allow the dam to stretch out comfortably, high enough to contain the puppies, and warm enough to maintain their body temperature.

your bitch is wormed and start constructing, or purchase, a whelping box. It should be large enough for the bitch to stretch out easily inside it. The sides should be high enough to keep the puppies in it while they are very young. For easy cleanup, line it with old towels, cloths, and newspapers — although the puppies may skitter across the slippery surfaces.

Find a quiet, warm, dry, and draft-free spot for the whelping box. Newborn puppies need a floor temperature of 85°F. (29°C.) to thrive during their first week, so warmth is important, particularly during the colder months. During the second and following weeks you can lower the temperature 5°F. (1.5°C.) per week until, by the sixth to eighth weeks, it is down to 70°F. (21°C.). Heating tiles, heating pads, or an electric light bulb help maintain the proper temperature. Finally, unless you make sure your bitch gets used to the box in advance, she may choose a more inconvenient whelping spot — a remote part of the cellar or a closet.

As the 58th day approaches, you may see indications that the birth is imminent — such as her pawing at the ground (part of her nesting instinct), general restlessness, and loss of appetite. At this point, do not leave the bitch in the house alone. About 24 hours before the onset of labor, her temperature will drop from the normal range of 100 to 102.5°F. (38 to 39°C.) to 99°F. (37°C.).

When Your Bitch Is in Heat

As she pants and strains to release the first pup, there may be some vomiting; unless it persists, do not be alarmed. As long as three interminable hours may elapse before the birth of the first pup — which is often the most difficult. First you will see the amniotic fluid, then the head, followed by the amniotic sac, which the bitch will break and eat. Then she will bite off the umbilical cord, and lick and massage the puppy with her warm tongue so that it begins to breathe, digest food, and eliminate wastes.

It is not unusual for her to eat the placental membrane as she warms the puppy and prepares it for suckling. Although this afterbirth is rich in protein and vitamins, it sometimes upsets the bitch's digestion. It is important to make sure that she discharges each pup's placenta, for a retained placenta can lead to a serious uterine infection.

Throughout the whelping procedure, make sure that only your family is present. I have seen a bitch arrest labor because she was alarmed by a strange voice. Next, make sure that each of the above stages proceeds. After the last puppy has emerged, remove the soiled newspapers and cloths and put down fresh ones. Once you are certain everything is clean and warm, dim the lights and let everyone — including yourself and your family — get some rest. Check the bitch and pups periodically, but do not disrupt the important bonding period between them. Do not be alarmed if the bitch appears rough at times; this treatment stimulates the pups' circulation and breathing.

There are instances, however, when you must become involved. If the bitch fails to break the amniotic sac, you must intervene immediately or the pup will die from oxygen depletion. Cut or tear the sac near the nose and strip it back over the pup's body. Swing it downward, supporting its head or — better yet, use a bulb syringe to remove any mucous secretions in the pup's mouth. Once its cry tells you it is breathing easily, briskly rub it with a soft, warm towel, and present it to its mother. If it has difficulty breathing, squeeze the chest cavity gently, first from side to side and then from front to back. If necessary,

position your mouth over its mouth and nostrils and exhale gently. If you breathe too vigorously, you may rupture the pup's lungs. Take your mouth away so that the pup can exhale. Gently continue until you see movement in its chest. Once it is breathing, return it to the bitch for nursing.

You may also have to help with the umbilical cord. If the bitch does not shred it properly, either because she bites it too cleanly or cuts it too close to the pup's navel, it may continue to bleed. You must close the cord off in the middle with a clamp or pliers, and remove it with a pair of scissors about 2 inches (5 cm) from the abdomen. Use a thread or some unwaxed dental floss to tie the stump; cauterize the wound with a disinfectant like iodine to prevent infection.

Finally, in between births, you may have to put the puppies on the nipples. This helps both the puppies and their dam; the sucking starts the flow of her first milk, the colostrum. It contains protective antibodies that ward off infectious diseases to which the dam is immune. Colostrum lasts no more than two weeks, and every pup should receive some during its first 24 hours.

Sometimes, when the dam has a large litter or when she becomes exhausted, she may ignore one or several puppies. If this happens, just make sure all the pups have received some colostrum. Do not try to foist them on her at this point. Instead, clean them, dry them, massage them, and keep them warm. If necessary, get some formula (see page 50) and feed them from a bottle yourself.

There are also a few instances when you must get advice from your veterinarian, either over the telephone or in person. These include the following:
• Your bitch shows signs of excessive pain or is trembling, shivering, or on the point of collapse.
• She has been straining for two hours and has not yet delivered her first pup.
• You notice a dark green or bloody fluid *before* the first puppy arrives. This means the puppy is not getting any oxygen because the placenta has separated from the uterine wall. After the first puppy,

this is the normal color for such fluid.

• A three-hour interval between puppies may be a sign for concern. Puppies should come at any interval between 15 minutes and two hours.

Normal whelping is truly an extraordinary experience, albeit not always a smooth one. In the end, the dam, the puppies, and you will all feel proud. Remember, though, that your veterinarian should check mother and pups during the 24 hours after they have settled in.

Puppy Care

The stage is now set for a glorious time with "your" litter. There may be minor irritations with a sometimes reluctant mother. There may be anxiety and pain at the loss of a pup and the inevitable parting as they move on to new families. But, on balance, the drama is an exhilarating one.

Act I: The First Three Weeks

For about the first two weeks a puppy's eyes are closed and they are unable to hear, so you and the dam have some extra responsibilities. Mostly, puppies "follow their noses," knowing instinctively where to find their mother's nourishing milk and how to nuzzle for warmth. Your bitch hovers close by; she nurses them, washes them, and cleans up their wastes.

At this point, the mother requires extra rations to provide for her brood. If it is a large litter, you may have to provide supplemental rations. Your veterinarian will advise you regarding frequency of feeding, types of commercial formulas available, and quantity to feed. You can also make your own formula. In an 8-ounce (227 g) container, mix five parts evaporated milk to one part water and add the yolk of a raw egg. Refrigerate until needed; serve at 100° F. (38°C.). Feed in a baby bottle with a nipple whose opening is wide enough for the pup to suck comfortably. Stop when it is no longer eager to feed.

The weaning process usually begins at about two to three weeks. Your bitch may offer the pups her regurgitated dinner. Do not be alarmed at this. It is a good way to accustom the puppies to the warm, mushy diet they require — even if you do find it unappetizing. At this point the puppies need plenty of water, so keep the water dish clean and fill with fresh water often. If the bitch cannot provide enough food for all the pups, add some oatmeal to equal parts of evaporated milk and water, plus the egg yolk, to achieve a gruel-like consistency. You can help the pups accept this food by dipping your finger into it and dabbing a bit on each puppy's nose. They will get the message quickly.

Because the puppies' tired mother may not be up to it, you may have to take over the grooming functions. Once the litter is awake and interested in food, make sure their eyes are clean and check their coats. The warm atmosphere may dry them out, so you can rub in a tiny bit of baby oil. After they have fed, a gentle massage will insure elimination, encourage circulation, and serve as exercise. Ask your veterinarian if this is the time to first worm the litter.

The most exciting, dramatic event occurs toward the end of the second week. You may come down one morning and realize to your amazement that one puppy is no longer blind. In short order, all the puppies' eyes open. Suddenly the passive mass of puppies becomes a flurry of activity. Perhaps most gratifying is the fact that they bring you into their world: they know your smell, your voice, and your touch. Their motor coordination increases rapidly and they are genuinely responsive.

Act II: From Three to Twelve Weeks

This act begins in comedy. Puppy play is a delight! You may watch a long-standing ritual of boisterous mock-battles and rowdy wrestling matches. You can see them act out scenes of stalking, chasing, pouncing, shaking, and biting their prey, which may be nothing more than a tennis ball, a forgotten leather glove, or a smelly sock.

As the puppies become more aware and respon-

When Your Bitch Is in Heat

sive, their mother gradually begins to withdraw from them. Her withdrawal increases their need to fend for themselves, which they must do at this point in their lives. Now they will become loyal to humans — first in your household and then in someone else's. You can best cement this bond by loving them and frequently handling them. Remember, it takes two to bond, and your role is important.

At this point, begin strengthening their teeth by giving them hard rubber toys or rawhide bones to play with. This is also the time to worm them — and their mother — again.

As in all good comedies, however, there is a tinge of sadness in this act. Between the eighth and tenth weeks, your litter must, quite literally, go out into the world. You must prepare for their departure by checking with your local chow club, your veteri-narian, and your friends. Do everything possible to insure that your puppies find warm, loving homes. Whether or not to keep one puppy is a family decision, which should be based on a frank assessment of your ability and desire to cope with another mouth — both to feed and to listen to — around the house.

Act III: Three Months and Beyond

This is the puppy's adolescence — a time of expansion. Both you and the dog will need patience. Changes in diet, temperament, and skills will keep you involved in the puppy's life. Introduce obedience training into the daily routine at this point. Specific suggestions and guidelines are found in the last chapter of this book.

In Sickness and in Health

Your chow chow's health is largely your responsibility. The chapters on diet, care, and understanding your dog have given you general guidelines. This chapter will give you specific information about health problems that may affect your dog.

If you suspect your dog is sick because you notice something unusual about its behavior, appetite, or appearance, get in touch with your veterinarian immediately. Your veterinarian is best qualified to diagnose and treat your dog.

Whether you are a first-time dog owner or have been around many of them, chances are that you will know when you should be concerned about your dog's health. Part of the bond between humans and animals is the sense that something is not right. It is similar to a parent's sense that something is not right with a child.

Often you will sense a problem because your dog is off its feed, is listless, has a problem with elimination, or has a dull look to its coat or about its eyes. Trust your instincts and call your veterinar-

The chow chow's musculature emphasizes the breed's strength and solidity.

ian. Even if your veterinarian is not immediately available, almost all will refer you to a colleague. Large urban and suburban communities have 24-hour veterinarian services. These clinics are a great comfort if you are ever faced — late at night — with a raccoon slash across an ear, a muzzle full of porcupine quills, or an ingested object.

Let us first consider the important health questions of puppyhood. These include vaccinations, internal parasites — worms, and external parasites — fleas and ticks. This chapter aims to start you on a schedule of preventive medicine. When you see your veterinarian for a periodic check-up, ask about feeding or any other concerns you may have.

Infectious Diseases

Bacteria and viruses are the most common causes of infectious diseases. They are usually

The chow chow's major bones and joints.

transmitted from animal to animal through contact with bodily secretions. As previously mentioned, the dam gives her pups immunity from many infections through her colostrum (first milk). In addition to this passive immunity, pups acquire active immunity through vaccinations.

Vaccinations

Adhering to a strict vaccination schedule will help you protect your dog against potentially fatal diseases. The five serious canine diseases are distemper, a systemic disease caused by a virus; parvovirus, an infection of the gastrointestinal tract; hepatitis, a viral disease of the liver; leptospirosis, a bacterial infection of the kidneys; and rabies, a viral disease of the nervous system. The last two diseases are potentially dangerous to humans as well. In fact, if either you or your dog has had contact with an animal presumed to be rabid, most states require that your dog be quarantined and that you undergo a painful series of shots. When you get your puppy, be sure to obtain its vaccination schedule so that your veterinarian can follow through with it. If the vaccination schedule is unavailable, contact your veterinarian and begin a schedule. The following chart suggests the age at which various vaccinations should be administered. Remember, however, that vaccination schedules vary according to the type and combination your veterinarian uses. Furthermore, your geographic location and the characteristics of the breed must also be considered. Your veterinarian should have the final say about the schedule.

As long as you adhere to the vaccination schedule, you need not concern yourself with detailed descriptions of these diseases or their symptoms. There is a variety of vaccines for some of these diseases as well as various strengths for the injections. The prevalence of these diseases in your community must also be considered. Your veterinarian can best advise you on these matters.

Age	*Vaccination*
5–8 weeks	Canine Distemper/Hepatitis/ Leptospirosis (DHL), Measles, Parainfluenza (Kennel Cough), and Parvovirus (Enteritis)
at monthly intervals until 12 months	DHL, Parainfluenza, Parvovirus and six monthsrabies Rabies
12 months and annually	DHL, Parvovirus, and Parainfluenza
three-year intervals	Rabies

Parasites

Many types of organisms and insects feed upon a dog's body. The presence of parasites, particularly in the intestines, does not necessarily mean disease. The following parasites can directly threaten your dog's — and sometimes your own — health.

Internal Parasites

Be sure to ask your breeder what worming procedures your puppy has had. If it hasn't been wormed, your veterinarian will ask you for a stool sample. *Hookworms* and *roundworms* commonly occur in puppies; the latter can also be transmitted to children. The roundworm, a yellowish-white worm 2 to 4 inches (5 to 10 cm) in size, inhabits the puppy's small intestine. It is important that you follow a proper worming schedule to spare your puppy needless suffering. Symptoms of a roundworm problem include weight loss, dull coat, prolonged diarrhea, cough, and vomiting.

Tapeworms and *whipworms,* on the other hand, affect older dogs. You may find detached fragments of tapeworms in your dog's bedding or in its stool. Whipworms are even smaller; like tapeworm

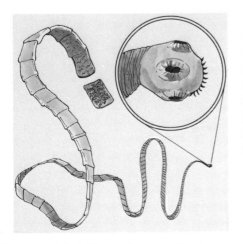

The tapeworm's body is long and segmented. Suckers on the head (magnified) enable the tapeworm to attach itself to the intestinal wall.

segments, they may look like grains of rice in a stool. Whether or not you have fed your dog rice, your veterinarian should check the dog. Although supermarkets and pet stores sell worming medication, it's better to get advice and medication from your veterinarian.

By far the most dangerous internal parasite is the *heartworm.* It can grow as long as 14 inches (36 cm) and attacks a dog through mosquitoes that act as the host for heartworm. It can take as long as four months to begin attacking the dog's heart or lungs. Veterinary medicine has recently made great strides in combating this deadly parasite. In early spring your veterinarian should draw a blood sample from your dog to be sure it is not infected. Then your veterinarian will prescribe daily medication, although a monthly liquid dosage is now available in some areas. Follow this procedure until you are sure that a killing frost has eliminated the host mosquitoes. Giving the dog preventive medication while it is infected can lead to death.

Despite the fact that one of my dogs was given preventive medication, it still developed heart-

worm. I spent an anxious three weeks until the dog was cured. Under the care of a competent veterinarian, a dog can survive heartworm. Preventive care, however, is a much better method.

Ringworm is not a worm at all; rather, it is a skin disorder caused by a fungus that penetrates the dog's skin. It forms small, sore rings or circles that are raised and filled with pus; they cause severe itching and inflammation. You must get your dog to the veterinarian quickly because this disease is readily communicable to humans — particularly children who cuddle the puppy or dog. Furthermore, it is persistent: clumps of hair from an infected dog can reactivate the fungus weeks or months later.

External Parasites: Insects

Many people believe that they must become resigned to *fleas* in summer. Chances are that your chow will be plagued by fleas at least once a summer, but do not stand idly by. Fleas carry diseases, act as a host for tapeworms, cause hair loss and skin irritation through the dog's scratching, and are a household nuisance if they enter your home through your dog.

Fleas love the chow's thick, multi-layered coat. Therefore, watch for them during grooming. If your dog has been attacked, you may see fleas jumping erratically through its coat, or you may notice black and white grains about the size of grains of sand on your dog's skin. These grains are flea feces or eggs. Eggs can turn up on your furniture, carpet, car seats, or your dog's bedding. Within eight days these eggs equal more fleas.

You will need vigilance as well as medication

Obedient chows are a delight not only to the owner enjoying a quiet moment with her pets, (above) but also to the owners preparing their potential champions for a dog show (below).

In Sickness and in Health

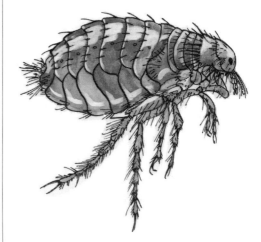

Fleas (magnified), which cause intense itching, can also serve as intermediate hosts for tapeworms.

The life cycle of a tapeworm. One type of tapeworm is transmitted by a flea that your chow has bitten or eaten, for immature tapeworms live in the flea's intestines.

from your veterinarian to cure a flea problem. Flea collars and other supermarket products may help, but they rarely stop the infestation. Because of the thickness of a chow's coat, a flea spray, or preferably a dip, may minimize your dog's flea population. In addition to the ultrasonic collar with a lithium battery mentioned earlier, your veterinarian now has a product that can be applied directly to the dog's skin. It will keep your pet free of fleas for a two-week period. If fleas have infested your house, use your vacuum cleaner to attack the eggs. If this does not work, contact an exterminator.

Ticks are another external parasite that make dogs and their owners miserable. Although they are found in forests, they are also found in many other places. They are related to spiders and appear flat—about the size of a match head. They cause a variety of diseases dangerous to humans, the worst being Rocky Mountain Spotted Fever and encephalitis; some have a toxin that can paralyze dogs. Adult ticks cling to a dog and mate. The female penetrates the dog's skin surface and sucks its blood. Soon the tick becomes bloated enough for you to remove it; however, it is easier to remove both male and

A watchful, alert, protective chow demonstrating some of the breed's outstanding characteristics.

Ticks (magnified) before (left) and after (right) feeding.

female ticks before they have become embedded.

Remove all ticks quickly. Although some people prefer to kill the tick prior to removal, that is not necessary. Soaking the tick with nail polish remover or alcohol first will choke off its oxygen supply and kill it. In any case, pull the tick straight up and out with tweezers, pliers, or your fingers. To make sure that you do not leave any part of the tick's head inside your dog where it might fester and swell, give the tick a few backward and forward twists while you gently extract it. If your dog is heavily infested, you will need a chemical dip from your veterinarian. If a swollen tick drops off your dog, this may mean trouble. Ticks carry countless eggs which, when hatched, can multiply your dog's problems rapidly. If you suspect this, see your veterinarian right away.

Mites are another type of insect parasite that may infect your dog. Mange and ear mites are the most common problems. Scabies or sarcoptic mange causes intense biting and scratching. The disease begins either with red spots that become pus-filled through scratching, or with dry, patchy, yellow-gray scabs. These usually appear around the dog's ears, head, neck and forelimbs; untreated, scabies can cover the entire body. Sometimes scabies is communicable to humans. Your veterinarian will probably treat it with an insecticidal dip and Panalog, an antibiotic ointment. Scabies takes a long time to cure because the treatment kills the most recent crop of mites, not the eggs themselves. Similar treatment is also prescribed for two other types of mange. One affects puppies and is called "walking dandruff." It is spread by a red mite and can be detected by unusually heavy dandruff on the dog's head, neck, and back. A third kind of mange, the demodetic type, is caused by a microscopic mite that burrows into the hair and causes red skin and loss of coat. Demodetic mange is passed on to a litter through an infected dam, so have your bitch examined before breeding.

Another red mite, sometimes called a harvest mite, originates in the larvae of chiggers and can be found on the dog's abdomen after a romp in the

Carefully examine your chow chow's coat and skin to detect external parasites such as the louse (magnified).

woods. Its cure is similar to that for ear mites, which live in the ear canals and feed on the debris that collects there. They are a common cause of ear infections in puppies and dogs. Your veterinarian can supply the proper medication for them, but be sure he or she also shows you how to administer ear medication to your dog.

Fortunately, *lice* are not a prevalent nuisance. However, they also multiply rapidly, and they can infest your dog if not treated. Although well-cared-for dogs usually don't have lice, they may be transmitted by sickly strays. They often look like dandruff because the sand-colored eggs (or nits) remain on the coat. An insecticidal dip will usually rid your dog of lice.

Useful Home Health Care Techniques

Health problems that affect all dogs, regardless of their age, and useful techniques for providing home health care, are considered in the pages that follow.

Taking a Dog's Pulse

The best place to feel a dog's pulse is the femoral artery located in the groin. Lightly place your fingers along the inside of the thigh where the leg joins the body. Two other good locations are the rib cage over the heart and the front paw on the left, or heart side, just below the elbow joint. Although a chow puppy may have a faster pulse rate, an adult chow

The proper way to insert an unbreakable rectal thermometer when taking your chow's temperature.

has a rate of between 70 and 90 beats per minute; during sleep it may drop to 62. Since a dog's heart beats in an idling rhythm at rest, you can expect some deviation in pulse rate. A strong, steady, regular beat is ideal. An excessively fast heart rate may mean blood loss, dehydration, shock, fever, or anemia. A very slow or faint beat may indicate poisoning or heart disease.

Taking a Dog's Temperature

The average temperature range for dogs is from 100 to 102.5°F. (38 to 39° C.), although a puppy's temperature may run slightly higher and an older dog's may be slightly lower. Use an unbreakable rectal thermometer to take your dog's temperature. Shake the thermometer down below normal and lubricate the bulb end with petroleum jelly. Then raise your dog's tail and hold it firmly so the dog cannot sit down, insert the bulb into its anal canal, twisting the bulb 2 or 3 inches (5 to 8 cm) into the rectum, and hold it in place for two or three minutes. Remove the thermometer and read the dog's temperature. (If you own a bitch, be sure to insert it into the rectum, not the vagina.) If you use a breakable thermometer and your dog is nervous or restless — or if it sits down — the thermometer may break off. If this happens, don't probe for the broken end; rather, give the dog 2 teaspoons of mineral oil to ease elimination and notify your veterinarian. Just as a high fever indicates illness, a subnormal one signals hypothermia — a condition that often accompanies poisoning.

If your chow resists having its temperature taken, take a tip from your veterinarian — first lift the dog onto a table. In addition to giving you more light and better access to the dog, it seems to make even the most feisty dog more submissive.

Giving Medications

The most common medicines you will give your dog are pills, liquids, and suppositories. You may be surprised at how uncannily your chow defeats your every attempt to give it medication. A good trick is to wrap a pill in some hamburger or a piece of sausage. If your veterinarian gives you powders or liquids whose odors do not distress your dog, mix them into its food.

To give a pill, open your dog's mouth and place your thumb on the roof of its mouth. While exerting upward pressure, use your other hand to pull down on its lower jaw. Quickly toss the pill as far back on the center of the tongue as you can. If you place the

In Sickness and in Health

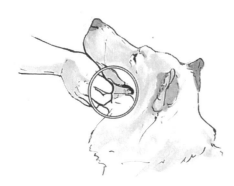

The proper way to give your chow chow a pill.

pill to one side, the dog can easily work it forward and spit it out. Close its mouth and keep it shut, while stroking its throat, until it swallows the pill. If your dog licks its nose, you will know you have succeeded.

For liquid medicine, ask your veterinarian for either a squeeze bottle with a spouted dispenser, a syringe, or an eyedropper. Tilt the dog's head at a 45-degree angle and squeeze or pour the liquid into the fleshy pocket at the side of its mouth between its molars and cheek. Seal the dog's lips around the dispenser and hold its muzzle firmly until the dog swallows. Never pour the liquid directly down its throat, no matter how adept you become, because you risk aspiration pneumonia.

Give suppositories the same way you take your dog's temperature, although you may want to use disposable plastic gloves. With one arm firmly around the dog's chest, insert the suppository as far into the anus as possible. You may need another person to help you support the dog's front.

You may have to give your chow an injection, particularly if it requires insulin. If this is the case, your veterinarian will prescribe it and instruct you in giving the injection. Again, you may need help. Another sound precaution is to muzzle the dog. Wind a gauze bandage, piece of cloth, necktie, stocking, or even a leash around the dog's nose and mouth. Do so firmly, but not tightly. Be sure to

carry it around the neck and head so that the dog will not be able to paw it off. Then follow the procedures demonstrated by your veterinarian. Do not attempt an injection without professional instruction.

For its patient and faithful execution of any one of these feats, your dog merits high praise. Perhaps even a treat is in order.

Home Health Care Checklist

In order to give your dog the best health care possible, you must maintain a close, working arrangement with your veterinarian. Nevertheless, there are instances when, as an informed owner, you can give your dog emergency first aid. The following list describes procedures recommended for a variety of situations. Of course, this information is not a substitute for your veterinarian's professional advice.

Note: Dosages are appropriate for a chow that weighs 30 pounds (14 kg). You may have to adjust them for larger dogs or puppies.

A muzzle full of porcupine quills is a painful experience. You may need your veterinarian's help to remove them.

In Sickness and in Health

CONDITION	TREATMENT
Abscess	Administer compresses of warm water and salt to prevent the abscess from enlarging and to allow it to drain until you see your veterinarian.
"Accidents"	A solution of water and vinegar is useful in cleaning up urine or feces. Water and household ammonia also help combat odor and discoloration.
Bad Breath	If it is caused by poor diet, give a solution of 1 tablespoon charcoal in 4 ounces (118 ml) water for several days — and, of course, improve the dog's diet (see pages 21-24). Check the teeth to see if tartar build up is the cause. Also, check for constipation or unusual stools. If you think it is more serious than a digestive upset, call your veterinarian.
Bee Sting	Apply a heavy paste of bicarbonate of soda or starch and, if your dog tolerates aspirin, give one to ease the pain. Check carefully for shock (pale gums, slow or weak pulse, shallow breathing, a glassy-eyed look, anxiety). If pain persists, call your veterinarian.
Bruise	Apply warm compresses; a puppy's bruise will normally heal easily.
Burns	A strong, cool tea solution is good for minor burns. If the skin is broken or there are blisters, use a cool compress dipped in a bicarbonate of soda solution. If it is a serious burn, call your veterinarian.
Collapse	Keep the dog warm with blankets until you reach your veterinarian.
Constipation	Occasional constipation is not serious; remove bones from the diet if it persists. One tablespoon milk of magnesia will relieve simple constipation. Rectal glycerine suppositories are also useful. Add mineral or vegetable oil regularly to your dog's diet to prevent constipation.
Convulsions	Remain calm and wrap the dog loosely in a blanket; then speak reassuringly to it. Never give your dog anything orally while it has convulsions — you may cause choking.
Cough, Wheezing, Sneezing	Familiarity with your chow will tell you whether or not these symptoms are serious. If your dog has a runny nose, watery eyes, or labored breathing, call your veterinarian.
Cuts	Your dog will lick small cuts to clean them. Treat larger cuts with warm compresses of salt and water and a mild antiseptic such as hydrogen peroxide.
Diarrhea	A watery stool for a day to two probably indicates mild digestive upset. Give the dog weak tea with a dash of salt instead of water. Also give a tablespoon of Kaopectate or a similar product every 4 hours. Because it may be a sign of worms, persistent diarrhea requires consultation with your veterinarian — along with a stool sample.

In Sickness and in Health

CONDITION	TREATMENT
Drowning	Grasp your dog by its hind legs so the water will drain out. If necessary, breathe into its mouth to stimulate respiration. Use blankets and a mild stimulant if the dog is conscious; use spirits of ammonia if unconscious. See "Shock" below.
Ear Problems	Rinse with isopropyl alcohol or soothe with a few drops of olive oil. Unless your veterinarian has instructed you, do not probe with a cotton swab.
Eye Problems	A gentle rinse with warm water will give relief. Call your veterinarian if you notice pus or any change in eye color. If you wear contact lenses use some of your own saline solution to rinse your dog's eyes. It does not sting as tap water does. Never use commercial eye drops unless your veterinarian prescribes them.
Fainting	This is more common among older dogs. Raise its hind quarters and keep it on its side so that it can rest. Do not give stimulants; call your veterinarian.
Fishhook Wound	Have your veterinarian remove an embedded hook. If not embedded, clip the hook's curled head and gently remove the hook. Use a mild antiseptic such as hydrogen peroxide to cleanse the wound.
Foreign Objects	If you know your dog has swallowed an object that you cannot dislodge, induce vomiting by putting 1 tablespoon salt on the back of its tongue. Call your veterinarian.
Fractures	If you think your dog has a fracture, do not move it. Gently transfer it onto a makeshift stretcher and transport the dog to your veterinarian immediately. Cover a compound fracture with gauze or a clean cloth. See "Shock" below.
Frozen Feet	Apply cold-water compresses and soothe with petroleum jelly.
Heat Prostration	Sponge cool water on the dog's facial area and feet. If the dog is unconscious, revive it with spirits of ammonia. Then give a mild stimulant, such as black coffee.
Hemorrhage	An arterial wound is one where you see spurting, bright red blood; place the bandage above the wound. A wound in a vein oozes slowly and the blood is darker red; place the bandage below the wound. You may need to apply pressure to stop the bleeding; however, never leave a tourniquet on for any length of time. You can stop most nosebleeds by applying an ice-cold compress.
Hip Dysplasia	HD affects the hip joint; the ball of the thigh bone, the femur, fits loosely in the socket and is thus not properly enclosed. Early signs, which appear in a puppy from four to nine months, include a limp, swaying gait, pain in the hip, or difficulty getting up. Eventually, HD causes painful inflammation similar to arthritis. In severe cases, surgical procedures may relieve pain and restore some function. The Orthopedic Foundation for Animals in Columbia, Missouri, will x-ray and classify any dog over 24 months for predisposition to HD. This is especially important if you plan to breed your chow. Pedigree papers should include its HD classification.

In Sickness and in Health

CONDITION	TREATMENT
Indigestion	If your dog shows signs of indigestion, stop feeding it for a day or so. Encourage liquids and when symptoms abate, begin feeding half rations of a bland diet. Resume regular feeding when the symptoms have disappeared.
Nose, Runny or Sore	Wrap some cotton around your little finger and swab the dog's nose; soothe with olive oil. If the problem persists, contact your veterinarian.
Poisons — Paint and Household Products	This is a serious problem and must be treated immediately by a veterinarian. If you know what the dog ingested, report it to your veterinarian. Treatment usually involves inducing vomiting, pumping the stomach, or neutralizing the poison. You can make an all-purpose emetic from 1 part milk of magnesia, 1 part strong tea, and 2 parts burnt toast crumbs. You can also try a tablespoon of salt on the back of the tongue. If you suspect strychnine poisoning, do not induce vomiting; rush your dog to the veterinarian.
Pills — Accidental Ingestion of	Induce vomiting, either through the above emetic or with salt on the back of the tongue. Follow with a mixture of an egg white in milk.
Porcupine Quills	If your dog's muzzle is full of them, see a veterinarian because it may require anesthesia, especially if the quills are inside the mouth. If you must do it yourself, sedate the dog, clip the end off the quill to reduce pressure on the shaft, and pull the quill straight out with pliers or forceps. then apply an antiseptic to the affected area.
Shock	If your dog has been hit by a car, it may go into shock — the signs of which are pale gums, shallow breathing, slow and /or weak pulse, glass eyes with wide open pupils, and anxiety. Since it will be upset and may behave unpredictably, reassure it, keep it warm, and transport it to a veterinarian on a makeshift stretcher as soon as possible. Give artificial respiration if it is not breathing; massage the heart if the pulse is weak. Keep the head of an unconscious dog lower than its body. Also, clear its air passage and keep its tongue to the side of its mouth.
Skunk	If your dog has an encounter with a skunk, give repeated baths in tomato juice or water mixed with vanilla extract to eliminate the odor. Although a dilute solution of ammonia in water may help, it also compounds the odors.
Snakebite	Quick action and a level head are necessary, especially if the snake is poisonous. Verify the bite: most harmless snakes leave horsehoe-shaped teeth marks — there are no fang marks. Fang marks indicate a poisonous snake. Because such bites are very painful, restrain the dog and keep it quiet. Struggling will make the venom be absorbed more quickly. Apply a tourniquet above the bite and loosen it for about half a minute every half hour. If ice is available, apply it to the wound. This lowers the dog's body temperature, retards the spread of the venom, and minimizes swelling. Use a sterilized blade to make parallel cuts across the swollen area, about ¼ - inch deep (.6 cm). Remove the venom with suction and take the dog to a veterinarian.

In Sickness and in Health

CONDITION	TREATMENT
Stomach Torsion	This serious condition usually affects a dog that exercises vigorously after it has eaten too much and/or drunk too much water. This gastric dilation can result in blocking of the esophagus and the duodenum. Immediate surgery can save the dog's life, but there is a 15 percent chance that it will recur.
Tonsillitis	Although dogs do not catch human-type colds, they can develop tonsillitis. Signs include vomiting of yellow phlegm, drooling, fever, and difficulty swallowing. Give your dog lukewarm tea until your veterinarian prescribes antibiotics.
Travel Sickness	If this recurs, ask your veterinarian for advice. Some prescribe dramamine or a tranquilizer, while others recommend a light meal and not too much water several hours before departure. In addition, do not feed your dog while traveling. Wait about an hour after your arrival before feeding.
Vomiting	It is not serious if your dog vomits occasionally after eating, as long as it maintains its appetite. If persistent vomiting occurs, call your veterinarian. You will have to describe the color and consistency so that your veterinarian will be able to advise you.
Vulva, sore	Because this may indicate a uterine infection, check with your veterinarian. Meanwhile, bathe with a mild solution of bicarbonate of soda in warm water every two or three hours.

In Sickness and in Health

Household Drug Dosages

Note: The following dosages are appropriate for a chow that weighs 30 pounds (14 kg). Adjust dosages for larger dogs or puppies.

Aspirin	One 5-grain tablet every 6 hours
Charcoal	One tablespoon in 4 ounces water
Cheracol-D (Cough Syrup)	One teaspoon every 4 hours
Dramamine	25 to 50 mg, 1 hour before departure
Hydrogen Peroxide 3%	Two teaspoons at 10-minute intervals, up to 3 doses, or until vomiting is induced
Kaopectate	Two tablespoons every 4 to 6 hours
Milk of Magnesia	One tablespoon every 6 hours
Mineral Oil	Two tablespoons
Paregoric	Two teaspoons every 8 hours
Tylenol	One tablet every 8 hours

Euthanasia

As difficult as this topic is, it is something you may eventually have to consider. Your veterinarian will describe the procedure objectively. You will have to consider the quality of life your dog will have. If it will suffer debilitating pain and if its prognosis is negative, the humanitarian thing will be to have the dog put to sleep. The injection of an anesthetic will lead to loss of consciousness and cardiac arrest. I have made this heart-wrenching decision three times; the last time I vowed never to own another dog. Happily, I subsequently broke my vow.

Training Your Chow Chow

The single most important rule to remember about training your dog is that you must first train yourself to train it.

People who assume that a chow chow is merely an esthetic object ignore the breed's history. They would mistakenly pamper and indulge a dog rather than put it through its physical and mental paces. Although the American Kennel Club assigns it to the non-sporting group of dogs, it has the potential to learn quickly and effectively. Do you have the will to elicit this potential?

Never Kowtow to Your Chow Chow

Your first instinct is to treat your new chow kindly — especially when it is a puppy. At the same time, your pet's first instinct is to look to you for guidelines about how to behave. If your leadership is absent, the dog's natural desire to play and please itself could take over. The result is likely to be that it will take a longer time than necessary to teach your dog how to adapt comfortably to your lifestyle.

Your new puppy, or even a recently acquired older dog, is not unlike a child in many respects. The desire to be a social being is fundamental to both the animal and the child. But they both need to be socialized. Each will accept its place in the family's pecking order, but neither can learn it on its own.

Furthermore, as is the case with children, there is no reason to believe that your life together should be an equal partnership. You must have a clear idea of what behavior is acceptable. It is your responsibility to teach your dog how to learn. Nevertheless, this is a cooperative venture; indeed, cooperation is one of your goals. Permissiveness, however, rarely makes a dog cooperative.

As previously pointed out, chow chows are more concerned with dominance than are most breeds. Typically, a chow may be out to show who's the boss if you are too permissive. Generally, chows need a great deal of praise during training sessions. Although your dog respects authority, you must strive for confident control — which a chow will respond to — and not an iron grip — which it will not. Therefore, train yourself to follow the rules in the next section, and you will be on the road to training your chow.

Remember, you are the dog's master, not the reverse. Should the tables be turned, you will suffer, your relationship with your pet will suffer, and, to make matters worse, ultimately your chow will suffer too.

You may hear that "you can't teach an old dog new tricks." This is untrue. Regardless of your dog's age when you acquire it, strive to establish the proper setting for the dog to learn your rules early in your relationship. You will be glad you did.

Discipline is the keynote for introducing a new dog to your rules. You need to consider what kind of training rules are necessary, how to apply them, and how to train your dog to be obedient.

Training Yourself

Before you begin training your dog, learn these five rules:
• Take your dog to the same place, indoors or out, for each training session. Find a quiet and fairly restricted location to avoid distractions.
• Begin training only when *you* are ready. If you're grouchy, you're likely to lose your patience and upset your dog. It won't understand what you want it to do, and it may begin to dread training sessions and to fear you.
• Work with your pet every day. Remember, though, that a puppy's attention span is short. At the outset, it's better to plan several sessions of about five minutes each than one longer session. As the dog matures, extend the session to 10 or 15 minutes.
• Decide what you want your dog to learn first. Then make sure your dog learns this well before

going on to the next lesson. Teach only one command at a time. It may take your puppy up to a week to learn it thoroughly. Remember, though, that how you teach your dog is crucial at this stage. Your intelligence in teaching is more important than your dog's intelligence in learning.

• Maintain a uniform attitude during training sessions. Your vocal commands and reactions must never vary.

This final point deserves elaboration. An authoritative, pleasant, consistent tone of voice will help your dog learn to associate its actions with what pleases you and with what angers you. Pitch your voice so that you consistently have a firm tone for commands, a sharp one for corrective reprimands, and a gentle, friendly one for praise. Your pet's response to your praise is wonderful to behold. It is important for developing trust between the two of you. It's easy to praise your chow chow when it follows your command. Remember, though, that corrections aren't always learned the first time. You may have to continue making the same correction. In any case, be sure to let your dog know that you appreciate its effort. This is not permissiveness; it's simply common sense.

It is most important for you to react *immediately* — with both voice and gestures — to whatever your dog has done. Your dog will not make the proper association if you continue to show anger long after it has misbehaved or not grasped your teaching point.

Note, too, that appropriate gestures are very important, for example, lowering your hand at the command, "lie down." Never hit your pet with your hand or with a folded newspaper, and never gesture as if you're about to hit it. Avoid having your dog associate a gesture with punishment. Using a folded newspaper, or the smacking noise it makes, is also counterproductive. You don't want to frighten your puppy with sudden or loud noises. Remember, scaring an animal into obedience isn't the same as teaching it. How often, finally, will you have a folded newspaper nearby? Certainly not at every moment when you want to reprimand your pet. The

associative learning typical of a dog occurs immediately, not half a minute later.

If your dog bites someone or is about to bite, you may be justified in hitting it. Nevertheless, consider carefully whether your pet's action deserves this form of punishment.

In order to succeed in training your dog, you must make the dog understand that an action on its part always produces the same reaction in you. Once this is established, mutual trust will develop between you. Also, your dog will learn the limits you have set, and it will develop security. Let's turn now to some helpful hints for applying these rules.

Training Your Puppy

As previously stated, your puppy will probably be at least eight weeks old when you acquire it. Wait until it is 10 or 11 weeks old before you begin training. A teething puppy is too young for a rigorous training schedule. However, your first two tasks are to teach it to recognize its name and to become housebroken. As soon as you get the puppy home, start calling it by its name as often as possible. If everyone calls it by the same name — and avoids nicknames until later — within several days the puppy will come when called.

Housebreaking

Housebreaking cannot be done casually or inconsistently. If you approach it this way, you will not be able to housebreak your puppy. You will not establish trust with your pet if you cannot trust it in your house.

Begin housebreaking by clearly teaching your puppy what is your house and what is its "house." Because a dog will not want to soil its sleeping and play areas, give your puppy a restricted zone for these activities — a crate or box with sides high enough to keep the puppy in it. Both you and the puppy need a sense of your space and what may be done within it. Once your puppy understands the

Training Your Chow Chow

Gentle pressure in both directions helps your chow chow learn the "sit" command.

boundaries of its house, help it learn the boundaries of your house. Then your puppy will know that although it may play in both areas, it must also keep both areas clean.

To teach your puppy what is your space, take it outside immediately after feeding it so it can relieve itself. Because your puppy also drinks water between feedings, take it out at regular intervals of 2 to 3 hours. Because the outdoors is a new space, with many intriguing scents, your puppy may not complete its task immediately. Males are particularly prone to dawdle. Thus, you must be patient, especially when it rains or snows. You must also praise your puppy generously — calling it by name — when it eliminates in the correct area.

It takes a puppy some time to develop control of its bodily functions. Accidents will happen. Despite your faithful attention, you may even suspect that its accidents are willful. Don't give up. Speak firmly but calmly to your puppy and take it outside immediately after an accident. The longer you wait,

the less chance it will associate your action with its action. Also, be sure to take your puppy to a location that it has previously used. In this way, your puppy's sense of smell will reinforce the lesson. Do not rub your puppy's nose in its wastes; this will not help discourage accidents. Once your puppy is housebroken, four or five outings a day should be sufficient.

If you live in an apartment, the early stages of housebreaking may be inconvenient. Your best method is to use newspapers. Choose an uncarpeted room such as the kitchen, spread open newspapers several layers thick around your puppy, and keep it confined to that area. Remove soiled papers as soon as possible and replace with fresh ones. Gradually reduce the covered area until the space is no wider than several open newspapers. If your pet soils the floor, speak firmly and gently place it on the papers so that it will realize that this is the area for elimination. Using a household disinfectant on the soiled area may not only clean it but also may be offensive enough to your puppy to discourage it from using that area again. By the time your puppy understands the limited area, it should be old enough for you to take it outside. Its sense of smell will help it understand that the outdoors is the proper area for elimination. You must, of course, maintain a regular schedule for these outings.

Whether you live in an apartment or a house, caring for your chow chow's needs at night is similar. Encourage bladder control by withdrawing the puppy's water dish a couple of hours before you — and it — go to sleep. Its final walk should be just before you go to bed. Place your chow firmly in its area, say "good night," and it will soon be able to control itself through the night. It will also be anxious for you to let it out first thing in the morning.

Begging and Being Alone

Your chow chow puppy should also learn these two lessons early. To discourage begging for food while your family is eating, feed your dog just prior to your own mealtime. As long as it smells food, of course, your puppy may try to wheedle a morsel from you with pleading eyes and a mournful whimper. Resist the temptation to feed it. Order it firmly out of the room or to its bed. Your clearing the table offers the puppy another begging opportunity. Although it is tempting to give your dog a few scraps, most veterinarians recommend not allowing your puppy to become used to a human diet.

Accustoming your puppy to being without you is another important, but painful, aspect of its early training. Begin by accustoming your puppy to short absences — go into another room so that it cannot hear or see you. Unless you prepare your puppy for being alone, it may become very destructive in your absence. Even after you have prepared the puppy to stay by itself, precautions are necessary when you begin to leave it for long periods of time. Leave the puppy in a room that is small enough for it to feel secure; be sure you leave it with fresh water, its bed, and some familiar toys. If it's not completely housebroken, spread some newspapers around. Also, be sure to remove sneakers and other shoes, rugs, books, upholstered furniture, sharp objects that could injure your puppy, and long curtains or drapes that it might rip or use as a swing in your absence.

You might leave the dog outside in the yard, but consider possible problems. A lonely puppy may begin to wail plaintively; this may upset your neighbors. You might let them know that the dog will be in your yard for a while. Also, neighborhood children may enjoy teasing your chow chow — and there's always the possibility of a dognapper making off with your cherished pet. If your neighbors are dog lovers also, you might ask them to keep an eye on your puppy while it is in your yard.

Collar and Leash Training

It's important for both you and your dog to learn how to use these items. You will need patience because puppies do not always want to learn what a collar and leash are for. But, because walks are an integral part of owning a dog, leash and collar training should be as pleasant as possible for both of you.

Your puppy will need two collars: an ordinary one, that may have its identification and rabies vaccination tags attached to it, and a training collar, better known as a choke collar. To determine the size collar your puppy needs, measure its head at its widest point and add about an inch. Put the ordinary collar on as soon as you bring your dog home; the younger the puppy, the less aware it will be of the collar. Let the puppy get accustomed to wearing it for several days before attaching a leash. When you do so, let the puppy drag it around until it becomes familiar with it. Make sure the puppy doesn't become entangled in the leash and so become frightened. In a day or two, begin holding on to the leash and walking with the puppy, but at this point don't start trying to train the puppy to follow your lead.

As has been mentioned, a teething puppy is too young to begin serious training. Learning to walk and follow directions on a leash are part of its earliest serious training. You should begin, however, only after you've introduced your chow chow to the training or choke collar. A choke collar is made of small, metal chain-links and has a metal ring at either end. You may find using a choke collar a little tricky at the outset, so first experiment with it off the puppy. Stretch the chain vertically with one ring in each hand and drop the chain through the bottom ring until the top ring meets the bottom one. Now that you have a loop, put the collar around your arm and tighten it by pulling upward on the top ring; loosen it by reversing this motion. When you are comfortable with this procedure, try it on the puppy — substituting its neck for your arm. Approach the puppy's muzzle head on. Holding the choke collar in front of the dog, form a loop and slip it over the muzzle and head so that both rings are on top of — not under — the dog's neck. Make sure you attach the leash to the top ring. (If you're right handed, the top ring should be in your left hand.) With the leash in this position, the slightest snap or tug will tell the dog the direction in which you want it to move. You can guide the puppy to the left, the right, or straight ahead. Of course, you must release the pressure as soon as your dog responds correctly; this will release the tension and teach the dog to follow your guidance in order to avoid discomfort and pain. If your dog is stubborn, you may have to repeat your guiding directions often. However, don't increase the pressure unduly. This will only cause your puppy unnecessary pain and make the training sessions distasteful. With proper discretion, your puppy's basic training will proceed successfully.

The Five Steps of Basic Training

You will be surprised how much fun your dog will have if you proceed properly with its basic training. Usually your dog will communicate its enthusiasm to you. Soon you will look forward as much as it does to the training sessions. The important thing to remember is that, although you can vary the order in which you teach your dog the following steps, you must concentrate on only one step at a time.

Begin by setting aside a period of about 10 to 15 minutes twice a day. Gradually extend the period to half an hour as you observe your puppy's attention span increasing. Select an area with few distractions — either from your family or from other noise. Your dog will soon realize that this is a special time, separate from its regular routine. Nevertheless, remember that you are teaching your dog to execute your commands at all times, not only at training time. Thus, training sessions must be fun, but they must also be controlled. Take the no-nonsense approach, yet combine it with plenty of praise as you sense your dog learning the commands. Always remember that you are training an animal, not a person. Your sessions will run more smoothly if, during moments of extreme frustration, you remember that animals are not naturally spiteful, obtuse, or vindictive. Indicate the end of the session by altering the pitch of your voice and by encouraging your dog to play and have fun.

When you give commands, be sure to distinguish between those that require movement and those that do not. For stationary commands or for the dog to be still, merely state the command ("sit," "stay"). For commands requiring movement, first get your puppy's attention by saying its name; then wait a split second and give the command ("Rover, come").

The Sit and Approval Commands

It's best to teach your dog the sit command at mealtime. Combine it with teaching the word or words you use for approval: "all right," "okay," or "yes." Place the food in front of the dog and apply steady but gentle pressure to its rump while saying slowly and kindly "si-i-i-it." Once it is in the sitting position, give it your approval to begin eating by saying "all right" or something similar. In addition to learning discipline, your puppy will learn not to take food from strangers, because it will associate "all right" with your giving it its food.

Down and Lie Down

Puppies and dogs are especially offensive both to their owners and to other people when they climb on furniture or people. As with all instruction, you must show your disapproval the moment your dog commits the act, in order for it to learn effectively. If you enter a room after the dog has stretched out on your bed, curled up in your favorite chair, or cuddled on the sofa, the dog will not associate its act with your disapproval. Wait until you catch the dog in the act. Say firmly, "Rover, down," making it your point perfectly clear through your actions and tone of voice.

Because your puppy or dog is likely to climb on you to show affection — especially when you return from an absence — disciplining it at that moment won't be pleasant. But you must do it. Otherwise, your dog will continue to behave this way — toward you and others. Again, a firm, clear, "Rover,

Training Your Chow Chow

Reinforce the "lie down" command by lifting the dog's front feet slightly off the ground and extending them in front of it.

down" should make the point. After the dog obeys, you show it that you accept its affection by bending down to its level. This will reassure your dog that you still love it.

It's also important for your dog to understand the command to lie down. A good time to teach this command is when the dog is tired, say after a walk or vigorous exercise outdoors. Although your puppy will eventually lie down on command, start teaching this lesson from the sitting position. Kneel alongside the dog, reach over its neck, and gently take hold of both legs at the elbow. As you lift its front feet off the ground and extend them slightly in front, hold the puppy there momentarily to calm it. Then ease it into the lying position, saying firmly, "Rover, lie down." Put some pressure on its hindquarters so that its haunches are underneath at an angle rather than straight. Otherwise it might try to brace itself to push off into the sitting or standing positions. Once the puppy is in the lying position, showly move your hand up its leg so that you exert a slight pressure on its shoulders. This will keep the dog from struggling; also cradling it in your arms will both reassure it and keep it from trying to brace itself with its front legs.

There are two important parts to this lesson: when you gradually ease yourself into a standing position and when you gradually move away from the puppy. It will probably try to follow you on both occasions. If it does not stay down while you are getting up, firmly press it down and say, "No, Rover, lie down." If your dog continues to get up, start the lesson over again. When it finally stays down, gradually lengthen the time it remains down until you reach a minute or so. Remember, though, that this is a long time for your dog. Then test your puppy by deliberately moving away slowly. Now it's time to teach the "stay" command.

Stay

This is a hard lesson to learn because it goes against your chow chow's natural inclinations. You can teach it from the lying down, sitting, or heel position; the latter is learned next. It often helps to accompany the direction "st-a-a-y" with a hand gesture, such as a raised index finger, which you can use with any verbal command in order to catch the puppy's attention. Another effective gesture is to bring the open palm of your hand down sharply in front of the dog's muzzle — but not hitting it on the

The "stay" command takes time to learn because it goes counter to your chow chow's wishes. Do not try to teach it early in its training sessions.

71

Training Your Chow Chow

muzzle — in a swift, chopping motion. At the same time, utter the "stay" command and gradually move away from the dog. When you begin teaching this command, stay within the dog's sight. Eventually, though, you should be able to leave the dog upstairs on the "stay" command, go down to do a brief task, and find it there upon your return. By the way, you will find this command most useful when you are coming down the stairs in your house. You don't want a racing dog accompanying you down the stairs, nor do you want a dog to interfere with a child or older person trying to descend.

Heel

Once your chow chow knows how to walk on a leash properly, introduce this very useful command. When it is learned, your dog will walk close to your left heel on a slack leash, with its nose at about the level of your left knee. Attach the leash to the choke collar and hold it in your right hand. That way you can control the leash with your left hand, lengthening or shortening the leash as needed. Begin walking in a straight line. Every now and then say "Rover, heel" and pat your left leg. If your dog strains ahead, sharply jerk it back to the proper heel position with your left hand and slacken the leash immediately. If the dog drags behind you, snap the leash to your side. Never drag or pull the dog into position. The sharp jerk should be sufficient, especially if you jerk the leash forward if your dog lags behind and jerk it backwards if it forges ahead. Reinforce the command by continuing to walk forward, repeating, "Rover, heel" and patting your leg. Introduce the turn to the left or right gradually. Keep the leash tight and away from you so that it will not bump you. Say "Rover, heel" while you turn on your left foot and bring your right foot around in front. If your dog becomes tangled, say, "Rover, heel" and bump it with your knee as you jerk on the leash. The right turn is similar; however, remember that your dog has farther to go in this direction. Once your dog learns to "heel," it

You will find the "heel" command useful for walks and bicycle rides.

will follow wherever you go, trotting amiably at your left side on a slack leash.

Often it is convenient to let your chow go without a leash. Teaching the "heel" command will allow you to do this, but don't remove the leash until your dog executes the command flawlessly. Choose a location where your dog will not be distracted by noise. Remove the leash, walk ahead of the dog, and say repeatedly, "Rover, heel." When your dog knows the command, practice in areas with more distractions and noises. You know your dog is ready to go without a leash when it obeys you at such locations.

Finally, if you like to ride a bicycle and exercise your dog at the same time, you will find the "heel" command useful. For your dog's safety, ride with it on your right to protect it from traffic. You must have absolute control over your dog before you try this. Because you would have to dismount first, handling an emergency would be difficult. Begin on quiet streets and be sure your pace is not too taxing on your chow chow. The chow's hunting ability makes it a good companion on short bicycle trips.

Come

Although I have saved this command for last, you will probably use it earlier in training your chow, perhaps to break any of the previous commands. You may also need it to avoid a dog fight or other dangerous situation.

If you and your dog enjoy good rapport, it will usually obey this command eagerly. Because you want your puppy to enjoy coming to you, do not reprimand it for not heeding this command. So, before you begin this instruction, arm yourself with some treats to reward it with — and to reinforce the pleasure of your company — and an extra long leash or a long piece of clothesline (20 feet [6 m] or so). Let your dog wander off, sniffing to its heart's content. When you are ready, calmly say, "Rover, come" or "Rover, come here" and jerk gently on the leash. If your dog obeys, be lavish with praise, hand out a treat, and pet it. If it does not come, repeat the command several times while reducing the slack on the leash by coiling it toward you. You might say, "Good Rover" once you have hauled the dog to you, but withhold a reward until the dog obeys fully. It will probably take several days' repetition for your dog to master the "come" command. When it does, start teaching the command with your dog off the leash.

Tricks and Games

After you have completed your chow chow's essential training, consider teaching it some tricks and games for fun — or for showing friends and relatives how intelligent your dog is. Here are three that most dogs and their owners enjoy performing.

Shake

A puppy's paw is constantly in motion, slapping first at its littermates and eventually at you. When you begin to teach this command, pick up a flailing paw, say "shake," and give it a tug. Later, use the "sit" command and then push against the puppy's right shoulder with your left hand. As it raises its right paw, take it in your hand, shake it, then praise and reward the dog. You can also teach your dog to shake its left paw; teach this command by saying, "*other* paw."

Fetch

Teaching your dog to retrieve an object does not require much work. Most dogs love to fetch. It also provides exercise and will not tire you too much. Of course, it's a little harder to teach your puppy to relinquish what it has fetched. With your chow sitting by your side, throw a stick or tennis ball and shout, "Rover, Fetch!" Once your dog has the object in its mouth, have it return to your side with the "come" command, followed by the "sit" command. Place a treat where the dog can see it, so that while you are saying, "Drop it" or "Let go," the dog will go for the treat and drop the object. Be sure your puppy has a chance to enjoy the treat but also praise it for dropping the object. Hold up the object and praise the dog lavishly. You can gradually introduce the name of the object (ball, stick, newspaper, and so on), as you give the "Rover, fetch!" command. To teach the "carry" command at the same time, move back several steps as your puppy brings the retrieved object, say "Carry" and then reward it. By moving back farther, you will teach your dog the notion of "carrying."

Scent Discrimination

Your chow's hunting instinct will help it learn this task, which it will need if you plan advanced training. Your friends may even think you have taught your dog a magic trick. You may need a helper because you want your chow to sniff a variety of objects and select only the one you have touched. If you do it alone, use rubber gloves or long-handled pliers.

Once your dog has learned the "fetch" command, work on scent discrimination. Get about a dozen rawhide bones and tie different color threads to eight of them in order to distinguish them. Saturate the other four bones with your scent; carry them with you for several days, and rub them often. Start by using only two bones. Have your helper place the bone without your scent on it about 15 or 20 feet (5 to 6m) from your dog. Give the "stay" command, show the dog your bone, and let it sniff it, but do not let it take it into its mouth. Still giving the "stay" command, go over to the other bone and place yours alongside it. Now return to the dog, let it sniff your cupped hand and say, "Rover, fetch." After sniffing both bones, your dog should select yours and return it to you. If so, shower it with praise. If not, make the dog drop the wrong bone and show it the correct one. Gradually increase the number of bones one at a time, but never let your

scent get on the bones with threads. That way, you will know which bone is which!

You may have heard it said that "an obedient dog is a joy forever." The commands listed under basic training are there to further precisely that goal. They are what you will need to work on to coexist pleasantly with your chow. If both of you find yourselves adept at these exercises, however, bear in mind that you can easily go beyond them. What you two have practiced will prepare both of you for a series of items that are required by the American Kennel Club as part of its Obedience Trials — one of the fastest growing branches of competitive dog sport. You might like to enter your dog in an obedience training class and take on the challenge of advanced training. Even if you do not choose to do this, take pride in the fact that your dog is now socialized. Whether or not you choose advanced training, you will enjoy living with a chow chow who responds instantly, alertly, and eagerly to a quiet word, a slight motion, or a click of the tongue.

Useful Addresses and Books

For Information and Printed Materials:

American Society for the Prevention of Cruelty to Animals (ASPCA)
441 East 92nd Street
New York, New York 10028

American Veterinary Medical Association
930 North Meacham Road
Schaumburg, Illinois 60173

Humane Society of the United States
2100 L Street N.W.
Washington, DC 20037

International Kennel Clubs:

The American Kennel Club (AKC)
51 Madison Avenue
New York, New York 10038

The Kennel Club
1–4 Clargis Street Picadilly
London W7Y 8AB
England

Canadian Kennel Clubs
111 Eglington Avenue
Toronto 12, Ontario
Canada

Australian National Kennel Council
Royal Show Grounds
Ascot Vale
Victoria
Australia

Irish Kennel Club
41 Harcourt Street
Dublin, 2
Ireland

New Zealand Kennel CLub
P.O. Box 523
Wellington, 1
New Zealand

The current Corresponding Secretary for the Chow Chow Club of America is:

Mr. Ernest Engberg
5022 Coney Weston Place
Madison, Wisconsin 53711

Since new officers are elected periodically, contact the AKC for the latest information.

For information about breed clubs and *Chow Life Magazine,* send $1.00 to:

Ms. Jill C. Stillwell
Route #3, Box 306-B
Dallas, North Carolina 28034

Useful Books

In addition to the most recent edition of the official publication of the AKC, *The Complete Dog Book* published by Howell Book House, Inc., 230 Park Avenue, New York, New York 10169, there are:

Alderton, David *The Dog Care Manual.* Barron's Educational Series, Hauppauge, New York, 1986.

Freund, Jan L. and Johnson, Dorothy L. *Chow Chow Champions*, 1952–1982. Camino E. E. & B., P. O. Box 510, Camino, California 95709.

Lorenz, Konrad Z. *Man Meets Dog.* Penguin Books, London and New York, 1967.

Smythe, Reginald H. *The Mind of the Dog.* Thomas, Bannerstone House, London, 1961.

Ullman, Hans-J. *The New Dog Handbook* Barron's Educational Series, Hauppauge, New York, 1984.

Index

Index

BARRON'S COMPLETE LINE OF DOG BREED OWNER'S MANUALS

Barron's *Complete Pet Owner's Manuals* include an extensive line of titles that provide basic information on individual canine breeds. The author of each manual is an experienced breeder, trainer, or vet. Each book is filled with full-color photos and instructive, high-quality line art. You'll learn what you need to know about each breed's traits, and get advice on purchasing, feeding, grooming, training, breeding, and keeping a healthy and happy dog.

Afghan Hounds
ISBN 0-7641-0225-7

Airedale Terriers
ISBN 0-7641-0307-5

Akitas
ISBN 0-7641-0075-0

Alaskan Malamutes
ISBN 0-7641-0018-1

American Eskimo Dogs
ISBN 0-8120-9198-1

American Pit Bull & Staffordshire Terriers
ISBN 0-8120-9200-7

Australian Cattle Dogs
ISBN 0-8120-9854-4

Basset Hounds
ISBN 0-8120-9737-8

Beagles
ISBN 0-8120-9017-9

Bernese and Other Mountain Dogs
ISBN 0-8120-9135-3

Bichon Frise
ISBN 0-8120-9465-4

Bloodhounds
ISBN 0-7641-0342-3

Border Collies
ISBN 0-8120-9801-3

Boston Terriers
ISBN 0-8120-1696-3

Boxers
ISBN 0-8120-9590-1

Brittanys
ISBN 0-7641-0448-9

Bulldogs
ISBN 0-8120-9309-7

Cavalier King Charles Spaniels
ISBN 0-7641-0227-3

Chihuahuas
ISBN 0-8120-9345-2

Chow Chows
ISBN 0-8120-3952-1

Cocker Spaniels
ISBN 0-8120-1478-2

Collies
ISBN 0-8120-1875-3

Dachshunds
ISBN 0-8120-1843-5

Dalmatians
ISBN 0-8120-4605-6

Doberman Pinschers
ISBN 0-8120-9015-2

Dogs
ISBN 0-8120-4822-9

English Springer Spaniels
ISBN 0-8120-1778-1

The German Shepherd Dog
ISBN 0-8120-9749-1

German Shorthaired Pointers
ISBN 0-7641-0316-4

Golden Retrievers
ISBN 0-8120-9019-5

Great Danes
ISBN 0-8120-1418-9

Greyhounds
ISBN 0-8120-9314-3

Huskies
ISBN 0-7641-0661-9

Irish Setters
ISBN 0-8120-4663-3

Jack Russell Terriers
ISBN 0-8120-9677-0

Keeshonden
ISBN 0-8120-1560-6

Labrador Retrievers
ISBN 0-8120-9018-7

Lhasa Apsos
ISBN 0-8120-3950-5

Maltese
ISBN 0-8120-9332-1

Miniature Pinschers
ISBN 0-8120-9346-1

Miniature Schnauzers
ISBN 0-8120-9739-4

Mutts
ISBN 0-8120-4126-7

Newfoundlands
ISBN 0-8120-9489-1

Pekingese
ISBN 0-8120-9676-2

Pomeranians
ISBN 0-8120-4670-6

Poodles
ISBN 0-8120-9738-6

Pugs
ISBN 0-8120-1824-9

Retrievers
ISBN 0-8120-9450-6

Rottweilers
ISBN 0-8120-4483-5

Saint Bernards
ISBN 0-7641-0288-5

Samoyeds
ISBN 0-7641-0175-7

Schipperkes
ISBN 0-7641-0337-7

Schnauzers
ISBN 0-8120-3949-1

Shar-Pei
ISBN 0-8120-4834-2

Shetland Sheepdogs
ISBN 0-8120-4264-6

Shih Tzus
ISBN 0-8120-4524-6

Siberian Huskies
ISBN 0-8120-4265-4

Small Dogs
ISBN 0-8120-1951-2

Spaniels
ISBN 0-8120-2424-9

Vizslas
ISBN 0-7641-0321-0

West Highland White Terriers
ISBN 0-8120-1950-4

Whippets
ISBN 0-7641-0312-1

Yorkshire Terriers
ISBN 0-8120-9750-5

Barron's Educational Series, Inc.
250 Wireless Blvd., Hauppauge, NY 11788 • To order toll-free: 1-800-645-3476
In Canada: Georgetown Book Warehouse • 34 Armstrong Ave.,
Georgetown, Ont. L7G 4R9 • Order toll-free in Canada: 1-800-247-7160
Or order from your favorite bookstore or pet store
Visit our web site at: www.barronseduc.com

(#110) 7/99

BARRON'S BOOKS FOR DOG OWNERS

Barron's offers a wonderful variety of books for dog owners and prospective owners, all written by experienced breeders, trainers, veterinarians, or qualified experts on canines. Most books are heavily illustrated with handsome color photos and instructive line art. They'll tell you facts you need to know, and give you advice on purchasing, feeding, grooming, training, and keeping a healthy pet.

Before You Buy That Puppy
ISBN 0-8120-1750-1

The Book of the Mixed Breed Dog
ISBN 0-7641-5065-0

Careers With Dogs
ISBN 0-7641-0503-5

Caring for Your Older Dog
ISBN 0-8120-9149-3

Civilizing Your Puppy, 2nd Ed.
ISBN 0-8120-9787-4

Communicating With Your Dog
ISBN 0-7641-0758-5

Compatible Canines
ISBN 0-7641-0724-0

The Complete Book of Dog Breeding
ISBN 0-8120-9604-5

The Complete Book of Dog Care
ISBN 0-8120-4158-5

The Complete Guide to the Dog
ISBN 0-7641-5204-1

The Dog: A Child's Friend
ISBN 0-7641-0302-4

The Dog Care Manual
ISBN 0-8120-9163-9

The Dog Owner's Question and Answer Book
ISBN 0-7641-0647-3

Dogs from A to Z: A Dictionary of Canine Terms
ISBN 0-7641-0158-7

Educating Your Dog
ISBN 0-8120-9592-8

Encyclopedia of Dog Breeds
ISBN 0-7641-5097-9

Fun and Games With Your Dog
ISBN 0-8120-9721-1

Healthy Dog, Happy Dog: A Complete Guide to Dog Diseases and Their Treatments
ISBN 0-8120-1842-7

How to Teach Your Old Dog New Tricks
ISBN 0-8120-4544-0

Hunting Dogs from Around the World
ISBN 0-8120-6632-4

Natural Health Care for Your Dog
ISBN 0-7641-0122-6

101 Questions Your Dog Would Ask
ISBN 0-7641-0886-7

Pudgy Pooch, Picky Pooch
ISBN 0-7641-0289-3

Puppies
ISBN 0-8120-6631-6

Saved! A Guide to Success With Your Shelter Dog
ISBN 0-7641-0062-9

Show Me!
ISBN 0-8120-9710-6

Train Your Dog
ISBN 0-7641-0967-7

The Trick is in the Training
ISBN 0-7641-0492-6

The Well-Behaved Dog
ISBN 0-7641-5066-9

Barron's Educational Series, Inc.
250 Wireless Blvd., Hauppauge, NY 11788 • To order toll-free: 1-800-645-3476
In Canada: Georgetown Book Warehouse • 34 Armstrong Ave., Georgetown, Ont. L7G 4R9
Order toll-free in Canada: 1-800-247-7160
Or order from your favorite bookstore or pet store
Visit our web site at: www.barronseduc.com

(#111) 9/99